1998

Garden Dreams

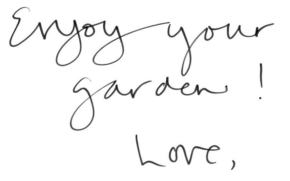

Dearest Angie,

Enjoy your
garden !

Love,

Ardie

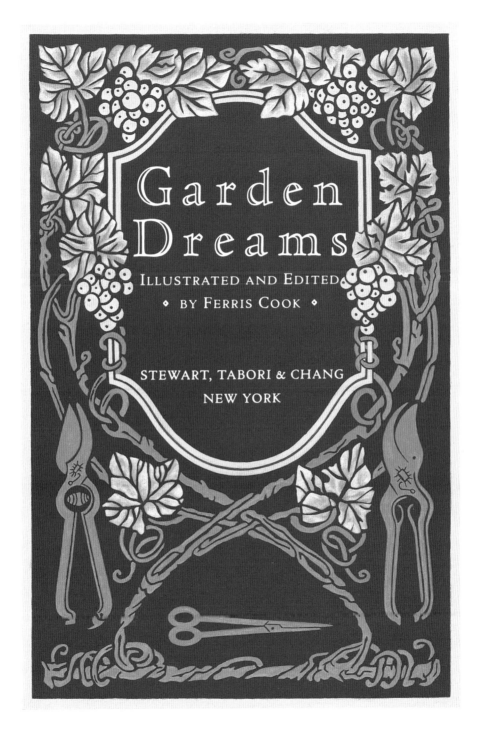

Garden Dreams

ILLUSTRATED AND EDITED
• BY FERRIS COOK •

STEWART, TABORI & CHANG

NEW YORK

All material by Ferris Cook copyright © 1991

Grateful acknowledgment is made for permission to reprint the following:

"A White Garden in Wales" from *What Happens in My Garden* by Louise Beebe Wilder. Macmillan Publishing Company, 1935, 1991.

"A Dream Garden" from *Home Ground: A Gardener's Miscellany* by Allen Lacy. Copyright © 1980, 1981, 1982, 1983, 1984 by Allen Lacy. Reprinted by permission of Farrar, Straus and Giroux, Inc.

"A Garden of Primroses." Reprinted with permission of Charles Scribner's Sons, an imprint of Macmillan Publishing Company, from "A Garden of Primroses" in *The Country Garden* by Josephine Nuese. Copyright © 1970 Josephine Nuese.

"A Garden of Paving Stones" from *Vita Sackville-West's Garden Book* edited by Philippa Nicolson. Copyright © 1968 by Nigel Nicolson. Reprinted by permission of Curtis Brown Ltd., London.

"Grandmother's Garden" from *Landscape Gardening* by Samuel Parsons, Jr. G.P. Putnam's Sons, 1891.

"If I Were Beginning Again." Reprinted with permission of Barrie & Jenkins, an imprint of Random Century, from *Gardens of Character* by Marion Cran. Copyright © 1940 Marion Cran.

"My Garden" from *The Education of a Gardener* by Russell Page. Copyright © 1962, 1983 by Russell Page. Reprinted by permission of Random House, Inc., and HarperCollins Publishers Limited.

"A Garden in the City" reprinted with permission of Henry Mitchell. Copyright © 1988 Henry Mitchell.

"If I Were to Make a Garden" from *If I Were to Make a Garden* by Ernest H. Wilson. The Stratford Company, Publishers, 1931. Reprinted with permission of Barbara S. Abbott.

Published in 1991 by
Stewart, Tabori & Chang, Inc.
575 Broadway, New York, New York 10012

Library of Congress Cataloging-in-Publication Data
Garden dreams / illustrated and edited by Ferris Cook.
ISBN 1-55670-172-1
1. Gardens.   2. Gardening.   I. Cook, Ferris.
SB455.3.G35   1991
712'.6—dc20   90-49054

Distributed in the U.S. by Workman Publishing,
708 Broadway, New York, New York 10003
Distributed in Canada by Canadian Manda Group,
P.O. Box 920 Station U, Toronto, Ontario M8Z 5P9
Distributed in all other territories by Little,
Brown and Company, International Division, 34 Beacon Street,
Boston, Massachusetts 02108

Printed in Italy

10 9 8 7 6 5 4 3 2 1

ACKNOWLEDGMENTS

If it weren't for the encouragement and support of many people, this book never would have been realized. I have worked with two wonderful editors, who deserve special thanks for their consistent and thorough involvement in every detail of the book. Brian Hotchkiss gave his time and energy generously as the idea of the book developed, and Jennie McGregor Bernard followed through as the pieces came together. I want to thank Andy Stewart for his appreciation of old garden books, and Kathy Rosenbloom for her meticulous care with the production. Diana Jones, the designer, and Wendy Wilson translated the vision we had of the book into reality.

Katherine Powis of The Horticultural Society of New York gave me unrestricted access to the books in their collection. And Bernadette Callery and her staff at the New York Botanical Garden Library were likewise patient with my request to pick books off the shelves according to design rather than name or title.

Also, I am indebted to two specialists in the garden book field. The late Elisabeth Woodburn of Booknoll Farm and Robin Wilkerson of Wilkerson Books gave freely of their time and expertise. The mornings I spent with each of them are most memorable.

On a more personal note, I would like to thank my sister, Sarah Longacre. She has offered a lifetime of guidance and friendship. And my husband and son, Ken and Isaac Krabbenhoft, who love books even more than gardens, have been my allies from the first summer in the garden. Ken has encouraged all garden expansion and book purchases, while Isaac has been my most enthusiastic art critic. With their company, I look forward to many happy years in the garden.

FOR MY
MOTHER AND FATHER

Contents

FOREWORD

Any book about gardens, written for the pleasure of writing, must have its sources in dreams. The visions of gardens beautiful and retired hover before the imagination, and no real garden, however humble, but is invested in celestial light of cherished hopes of what it may become in fragrant flowers or what it might have been had fortune been kind.

THE JOY OF GARDENS, 1911
Lena May McCauley

Gardening and dreaming have the same transitory quality that makes them hard to describe from beginning to end. Putting the two together in a garden dream is doubly illusive. My garden dream is as vivid as any dream, in the dreaming of it. But I carry only vague images into the waking hours: stone walls, great lawns, woodland paths, small pools, cascading roses, clematis, and an entanglement of other flowers as they transform through the seasons. When I enter my real garden I can't recognize much of the dream at all.

Only an experienced gardener can plant a whole garden in the mind's eye. For the rest of us, the garden seems to have a mind of its own. It starts with what is there, and incorporates what the neighbors offer, and plants from the library fair, and seeds, bulbs, and plugs from mail-order and local nurseries. It's more like a juggling act than a personal vision.

If your garden was there before you were, chances are it grew out of many others' dreams. I owe thanks to Fran for cultivating the birds and beebalm in my garden, Dan for the pear trees and yews, and Dick and his family for the quinces, peonies, and lilacs. Now I am contributing my part to this collective dream, with lots of help from my friends.

Because the garden dream is built primarily on memories, the remembered gardens of childhood are perhaps the most influential. The rose-shrouded trellises in my grandmother's garden formed a hidden clothes-drying room and one of my fondest memories is of fetching hot beach towels from that fragrant place, while watching out for bees and prickly grasses. Someday I hope to enclose a similar small space with some lovely old trellises I have stored away. From my great aunt, I inherited a love of early-blooming daylilies, and the rootstock of her plants now grows in my garden. And my enduring favorites, pansies, remind me of early spring outings to a nursery with my mother. We called these the trips to the Pansy Man, and it is still my spring ritual.

As the memories fade they are replaced by dreams, some realized, some vaguely desired. I've recreated a spectacular spring garden I once saw at the Brooklyn Botanic Garden: a skyrocket juniper, which rose in the center of a tulip bed, now stands surrounded by heathers in my garden. But a boxwood topiary garage, such as I saw in Portugal, wouldn't suit the climate here, nor would a picture-window terrarium go well with my old house. Are they in my garden dream, or not? I do dream of an enclosed garden, surrounded by climbing plants. It will have a high fence of unpainted and closely-spaced boards to shut out stray balls and wandering dogs. Where an immovable boulder prevents planting, there will be a pool with a rock island. And at the opposite end of the garden, I can see a wide and heavy gate, easy to swing open.

The garden writers collected in this volume cover a range of visions from pure fantasy to recollections of entire gardens. By recording their dreams, they have taken the transitory and illusive qualities of the garden and made a permanent vision. Perhaps these dreams will encourage readers to define their own garden plans, and to distinguish between real and imaginary expectations. I was inspired by Vita Sackville-West's dream, and have made a small paving-stone garden in a neglected spot by my cellar door. Happily, the garden grows slowly, and I have time to rearrange it all. Maybe my plans will give way to a greater dream.

High Falls, NY

A White Garden in Wales

Louise Beebe Wilder

T the center of each man's being, says Chester-
ton, is a dream. My pet dream for many years has
been a white garden, set apart and inclosed within
a shining green hedge. I never have come any-
where near to realizing this dream, never had space enough to be
anything so special—or perhaps it is horticultural self-control that has
been lacking. Something. But since the mild summer evening on which I
once saw a white garden beautifully carried out it has lingered in my
mind as indeed "such stuff as dreams are made on," and one of the
loveliest gardens I ever saw.

This white garden was one of a series of gardens on a splendid
estate in Wales, on the river Ely, not far from ancient Llandaff. It was
planted entirely with white-flowering plants and inclosed, not in the close-
clipped hedges of my desire, but by stone walls of a warm pinkish gray.
This was not, as might be supposed, cold in effect; the curious hue of the
stone was warm and almost luminous and made a delightful background
for the pale flowers. We saw this garden first at twilight, that witching

hour, and through the tall iron gates, above which swung a Clematis starred with immense white blooms, the effect was almost as if a mist had crept up from the river and finding the haven of this quiet inclosure had swirled around and about, rising here in wraith spires and turrets, lying there in gauzy breadths amidst the muted green. It is impossible to describe its beauty at this dim hour—so soft, so ethereal, so mysterious, half real it seemed. And yet when we saw it at noon of the next day it was no less arresting, though in a different way. It had become, so to speak, flesh and blood. Something you could draw boldly near to. Looking at it, we did not speak in whispers as we had done the night before.

Now it would be natural to suppose that a garden planted wholly with white flowers would be bleak in effect, or at least very monotonous; but this was not at all the case. It was neither funereal nor weddingish in appearance. It was frank and fresh and full of changing values. At twilight, of course, it seemed a little unreal, but isn't that true of almost any garden at this hour when the hand of man is less apparent and mysterious agencies seem to have brought it into being? There are, as a matter of fact, almost no *pure* white flowers. I have seen Sweet Peas of an absolutely flat paper-whiteness, but for the moment I can call to mind no other flowers of such unrelieved pallor. A large proportion of so-called white flowers tend towards buff, or mauve or blush in the throat; the petals of many are delicately lined, or veined or blotched with color— blue, carmine, green, yellow. A great number are not white at all but what we call cream-white, blush-white or skimmed-milk white, and the name of those having a greenish cast is legion. Many flowers change from white to pink or even to deep rose or yellow as they age, while bunches of bright-hued stamens or stigmata often cast a glow over the whole flower. Things being as they are, there could not possibly be monotony of tone in a garden of white flowers.

And there is besides infinite diversity of texture; there will be the flat sheenless whites, the satin whites, the velvet whites, while the variety of form is as great as among other flowers—spires, wedges, flat corymbs, spikes, bursts of mist, trails, streamers, banners, and plumes, they lie along the ground, aspire slenderly, climb the walls and trellises, are hung from tree and shrub in infinite multiformity and contrast. And in addition the foliage of the different plants and shrubs offers its own contrastive spice—the dark and light and yellow-greens with the many gray and silvery tones of the leaves quite preventing any monotonous duplication or harping recurrence of hue. It was plain, however, that this Welsh garden was the product of the most loving care and intelligent choice of material.

At the back of the garden, which was in the form of a large rectangle, a raised rectangular stone pool with a broad coping interrupted the wide border against the wall. The pool was lined with the palest sea-blue tiles, and out of a spray of carved (stone, I think) Lilies in the center a slender jet of water arose high in the air and swayed this way and that like a dancer in the wind, falling back finally with a light whisper into the clear waters of the basin. At the corners on the wide coping stood large tubs filled with white Lilies of the Nile.

The border that extended around the inclosure only interrupted by the pool and the gateway was about seven feet wide. The flowers were all congregated here, leaving the heavy velvet turf of the rest of the inclosure unbroken save that just off the center a very old Thorn tree spread its dark crooked branches, and in its shadow a little iron table and a few comfortable seats were casually placed. The suggestion of tea and pleasant loitering in this peaceful, fragrant spot was very agreeable.

It was midsummer when we saw this white garden in Wales, and the flowers that held the stage at this season were chiefly great masses of wedge-headed Phloxes, tall and dwarf, the tall spires of Chimney and other Bellflowers, Boltonias, white Lilies, annuals in a wide variety, including Sweet Peas that were supported on trellises at the back of the border, Gladioli and Dahlias, and a few shrubs. The borders were edged

with stone, and spilling over this confining band in masses were white annual Pinks, Phlox Drummondii, Cupflower, Petunias, frilly and plain, Verbenas, pale California Poppies, Sweet Alyssum, Carpathian Harebells, Heuchera, Flaxflowers, and the like. Here and there a climber came from the outer side and flung itself over the rim of the wall in tangled masses or long streamers, and more than one lingering Rose pressed a satin cheek against the warm-hued stone.

A chief and very apparent charm of this white garden was its sweetness, for many white flowers are fragrant, especially towards night. At dusk the perfumes arising from white Tobacco, Stock, Lilies, the masses of gray-white Heliotrope, Tuberoses, and Petunias were almost overpowering. And besides the fragrant flowers I noticed that a thoughtful hand had set among them plants of Lemon Verbena, Sweet Geranium, Southernwood, Rosemary, Lavender, *Cedronella triphylla*, and other plants beloved for their scented leaves.

We talked with the gardener in charge and learned that this garden was cunningly planted to be as full of bloom as possible throughout the season and not, as is often the case with one-color gardens, for a short period only. Many spring- and summer-flowering bulbs were made use of, a wide range of annual and perennial plants, shrubs, climbers, and trees of medium height and gracious blossoming. Various devices were employed to maintain the continuous bloom. Annuals raised elsewhere were transplanted to blank spaces left by departed bulbs and to fill other gaps in the flowery procession; Lilies and Heliotropes and Tuberoses in pots were dropped in wherever they would do the most good. All withered or spent plants were immediately cleared away and replaced by something fresh. The British are clever at keeping a border always appearing at the peak of perfection, and their climate is their ally rather than their antagonist in this worthy aim.

I sat on one of the white seats in the midst of this gracious garden and rested my notebook on the little table while the friendly gardener patiently enumerated the plants he made use of to keep the borders always fresh and blossomy. This list I have changed a little, adding a few special favorites of my own and omitting certain plants that are unsuitable to our more severe climatic conditions, or that are at the present time unprocurable in this country. I give it here for the benefit of any who may be cherishing a similar dream to mine, or who may here and now give birth to one. I am sure a little inclosed white garden, or even a winding border of white flowers against a green background, would be a possession of which one would not easily tire. It would always suggest peace and harmony, yet there would be no lack of interest. Frayed nerves would find it remedial.

Shrubs or Small Trees to Be Used
as Accents or Background

Spring-flowering: Amelanchier canadensis, 10 ft.; *Aronia arbutifolia*, 10 ft.; *Chamaedaphne calyculata*, 3 ft. evergreen; *Cornus florida*, 10–20 ft.; *C. Kousa*, 10–15 ft.; *Crataegus Oxyacantha* and *C. O. plena* (Hawthorn), 10–20 ft.; *Cytisus albus*, White Spanish Broom, 4–8 ft.; *C. kewensis*, low-growing; *Daphne Mezereum alba*, 4 ft. March; *Deutzia gracilis*, 1½ ft.; *D. Lemoinei; Exochorda grandiflora*, 10 ft.; *Halesia tetraptera*, 20 ft.; *Leucothoë Catesbaei* (evergreen), 4 ft.; *Lonicera bella albida*, 10 ft.; *L. fragrantissima*, 8 ft.; *L. Morrowi*, 12 ft.; *Magnolia conspicua*, 20 ft.; *M. stellata*, 8–10 ft.; *Philadelphus* (Mock Orange), many vars. tall and dwarf, single and double; *Pieris floribunda* and *P. japonica* (evergreen), 3–6 ft.; *Prunus glandulosa sinensis* (White-flowering Almond), 4–5 ft.; *P. maritima* (Beach Plum), 2–5 ft.; *P. tomentosa*, 5 ft.; *Prunus* (Cherry), Japanese vars., 20–30 ft.; *P. Persica flore-alboplena* (Peach); *Pyrus (Malus) baccata*, 20–30 ft.; *P. Sargenti*, 8 ft.; *P. toringoides*, 25 ft.; *Rhododendron carolinianum album*, 4–6 ft.; many hybrid vars.; *Rhodotypos kerrioides*, 5–6 ft.; *Rubus deliciosus*, 3–6 ft.; *Spiraea arguta*, 6 ft.; *S. prunifolia*, 6 ft.; *S. Thunbergii*, 3–5 ft.; *S. Vanhouttei*, 8 ft.; *Viburnum Carlesii*, 3–5 ft.; *V. Lantana*, 15 ft.; *V. Lentago*, 20 ft.

Summer- and autumn-flowering: Abelia chinensis, 4 ft.; *Calluna vulgaris alba*, 15 ins.; *Ceanothus americanus*, 2–4 ft.; *Chionanthus virginica*, 15 ft.; *Cladrastis lutea*, 50 ft.; *Clethra alnifolia*, 4–8 ft.; *Cornus Nuttallii*, 8–10 ft.; *Deutzia scabra (crenata)*, 8 ft.; *Hibiscus syriacus* Jeanne d'Arc (double), *H.* Snowstorm *(totus albus)* (single), 12 ft.; *Hydrangea arborescens grandiflora*, 5 ft.; *H. radiata*, 6 ft.; *Itea virginica*, 4 ft.; *Kalmia latifolia* (evergreen), 4–8 ft.; *Lonicera Ruprechtiana*, 12 ft.; *L. tatarica alba*, 10 ft.; *Rhododendron (Azalea) viscosum*, 4–6 ft.; *Rosa multiflora japonica*, 10 ft.; *R. rugosa alba* and vars., 5 ft.; *R. spinosissima*, 4–5 ft.; *Sambucus canadensis* (Elder), 10 ft.; *Syringa* (Lilac) *persica alba*, 8 ft.; *Syringa vulgaris* Frau Bertha Dammann, Marie Legraye, Jan van Tol (single), Edith Cavell, Mme. Casimir-Perier, Mme. Lemoine (double); *Viburnum americanum*, 12 ft.; *V. cassinoides*, 12 ft.; *V. tomentosum*, 8 ft.; *Weigela candida*, 7 ft.

Tall Plants for Use at Back of Border

Summer-flowering: Althaea rosea (Hollyhock), white vars., double and single; *Aruncus sylvester; Aster* Lady Trevellyn; *Bocconia cordata; Campanula lactiflora alba, C. pyramidalis alba; Cimicifuga simplex, C. racemosa; Delphinium*, white vars.; *Digitalis purpurea alba; Filipendula camtschatica (Spiraea gigantea); Iris ochroleuca (gigantea); Thalictrum aquilegifolium, T. cornuti, T. dipterocarpum album; Verbascum* Miss Willmott.

Fall-flowering: Aster White Climax; *Boltonia asteroides; Chrysanthemum uliginosum; Phlox* Jeanne d'Arc; *Veronica virginica alba.*

PLANTS OF MEDIUM HEIGHT

Spring-flowering: Aquilegia nivea; Astilbe japonica; Dianthus barbatus album (Sweet William); *Hesperis matronalis alba; Iris florentina* and intermediate vars.; *Linum perenne album; Polemonium caeruleum album.*

Summer-flowering: Achillea Ptarmica Boule de Neige, *A. P.* Perry White; *Astilbe* Gerba d'Argent, *A.* Moerheim, *A.*W. E. Gladstone; *Campanula alliariaefolia, C. latifolia alba, C. Medium* (Canterbury Bells), *C. persicifolia alba; Centaurea montana alba; Centranthus ruber albus; Chelone glabra; Chrysanthemum maximum* vars.; *Clematis recta; Dictamnus; Filipendula hexapetala* (Dropwort), *F. Ulmaria* (Queen of the Meadow), *F. purpurea alba (Spiraea palmata); Galega officinalis alba; Geranium pratense album, G. sanguineum album; Gypsophila paniculata,* double and single; *Iris* (bearded), many vars.; *Iris* (Japanese); *Iris sibirica alba* and vars.; *Lobelia siphilitica alba; Lupinus polyphyllus albus; Monarda fistulosa alba; Oenothera speciosa; Papaver orientale* Perry's White; *Paeonia,* double and single, many vars.; *Pentstemon digitalis alba; Phlox* Frau Anton Buchner, *P.* Fräulein von Lassburg, *P.* Mrs. Jenkins, *P.* Miss Lingard; *Physostegia virginica alba; Platycodon grandiflorum album; Sidalcea candida; Stenanthium robustum; Tradescantia virginiana alba; Veronica longifolia alba, V. spicata alba; Yucca filamentosa.*

Fall-flowering: Anemone japonica Richard Ahrens, *A. j.* Whirlwind; *Aster* Snowflake; *Chrysanthemum coreanum, C.* Hardy Japanese; *Eupatorium Frazeri, E. ageratoides; Hosta plantaginea grandiflora* (Plantain Lily).

LOW-GROWING

Spring-flowering: Aquilegia flabellata nana-alba; Arenaria montana; Arabis albida and *A. a. fl.pl.; Asperula odorata; Cerastium tomentosum; Convallaria majalis* (Lily of the Valley); *Dianthus deltoides albus; Epimedium macranthum album; Erinus albus; Gypsophila cerastioides; Iberis sempervirens; Iris,* dwarf vars.; *Myosotis; Phlox divaricata alba, P. subulata Nelsonii; Primula polyantha* (white vars.) *Sanguinaria canadensis; Silene alpestris; Statice Armeria alba* (Thrift); *Tiarella cordifolia; Veronica rupestris alba; Vinca minor alba; Viola cornuta alba.*

Summer-flowering: Anemone sylvestris; Campanula carpatica alba; Delphinium chinense album; Dianthus Her Majesty, *D.* Mrs. Sinkins, *D.* Bristol Purity; *Erigeron Coulteri; Galium boreale; Helianthemum,* white vars.; *Heuchera* Perry White; *Lychnis Viscaria alba; Nierembergia rivularis; Oenothera caespitosa; Phlox* Tapis Blanc, *P.* Mia Ruys; *Primula japonica alba; Scabiosa caucasica alba; Sedum album; Stokesia laevis alba; Thymus Serpyllum albus; Tunica Saxifraga alba.*

Autumn-flowering: Aster ericoides; A. ptarmicoides; Chrysanthemum arcticum; Helleborus niger.

Annuals for Summer-Flowering

(Only white-flowered forms of kinds named are intended)

Ageratum; *Alyssum maritimum;* Antirrhinum, tall and dwarf; *Argemone mexicana;* Asters, tall and dwarf; Balsam; Bellis; Candytuft; Sweet Sultan; Cornflower, double; Clarkia; Cosmos, early and late; Chinese Pinks; Godetia Duchess of Albany; *Gypsophila elegans;* Heliotrope White Queen; *Lavatera splendens;* Larkspur; Lobelia; Mignonette; *Nicotiana affins; Omphalodes linifolia;* Pansies; Petunia, double and single; *Phlox Drummondii;* Poppies; Scabiosa Shasta; Sweet Peas; Stocks; Verbena; Zinnias, tall and dwarf.

Spring- and Summer-Flowering Bulbs to Be Planted in Autumn

Allium neapolitanum, A. ursinum; Anthericum Liliago (summer); *Camassia Leichtlinii alba; Chionodoxa Luciliae alba; Colchicum autumnale album, C. speciosum album* (autumn); *Crocus biflorus, C. versicolor picturatus;* hybrid Crocuses (spring-flowering); *C. hadriaticus, C. speciosus albus* (autumn-flowering); *Eremurus Elwesii albus,* 10–12 ft.; *Erythronium californicum, E. giganteum; Fritillaria meleagris alba;* Galanthus (Snowdrop) species; Hyacinths, double and single; *Hyacinthus amethystinus albus; Leucojum aestivum, L. vernum; Lilium auratum* (summer), *L. Brownii* (early summer), *L. candidum, L. Martagon album; L. speciosum album* (late summer), *L. regale* (July); Narcissus, many vars.; *Ornithogalum umbellatum;* Tulips, many vars.; *Scilla campanulata alba, S. nutans alba, S. sibirica alba.*

Summer-Flowering Bulbs and Roots to Be Planted in Spring

Dahlias, tall and dwarf; Gladioli; *Hyacinthus candicans;* Tuberoses, double and single; *Zephyranthes alba.*

Climbers

Actinidia arguta; Clematis Duchess of Edinburgh, *C. Henryi, C. montana, C. paniculata, C. Veitchiana; Ipomoea grandiflora* (Moonflower); *Lonicera Halliana; Lathyrus latifolius albus; Polygonum Auberti;* Rose, many vars.; *Wisteria sinensis alba.*

A Dream Garden

Allen Lacy

E tell ourselves, and sometimes our friends, that when we moved into this house there was no garden here, as there is now, over a decade later. There was a front yard and a back yard and two side yards merging imperceptibly into both, but no flowers to speak of or shrubs of any particular interest. Today there are flower beds in respectable bloom from March till September. Some cotoneasters that I planted have now grown immense. They are a fine sight in early summer, when they bloom, attracting honeybees by the thousand and filling the garden with a sweet scent that stops just this side of sickening. Some of them have clusters of creamy flowers resembling bridal wreaths, except for being a kind of semi-virginal off-white; others bear much sparser clusters of tiny pink flowers that never fully open and that exude a sticky nectar enjoyed by several kinds of ants. It was a fine idea to plant crimson clematis beneath the cotoneasters, for they have clambered through the intricate architecture of their inner branches to emerge triumphantly on top with a profusion of blossoms in May and June and intermittent bloom

thereafter. I gladly take credit for my quince tree, though I'm not so happy with the two mock oranges I bought from the same mail-order nursery. Alleged by the catalog to be both double and extremely fragrant, they are unarguably single and have no more scent than cardboard. One of these days, when it stops sulking and begins to grow, I can show garden visitors a fine Japanese red maple. And most years, when the daffodils bloom I turn into a complete exhibitionist, inviting all the neighbors in to see them and coming close to putting up a sign in the street demanding the attention of strangers, too.

But the fact is that most of the decisions that have affected the character of my garden were made by other people, long before we bought this house. I did not plant the swamp maple that dominates the back yard, or the two old cedar trees that rise like exclamation points by the driveway and in the southwest corner of the front yard. The location of the perennial beds was determined by the sidewalks and hedgerows and fences that were already here when we moved in. Like many gardeners, I have a lazy streak. I wouldn't mind it in the slightest if some distant, unknown, wealthy kinsman should pass on to glory and leave me a sizable sum of money in trust, with the strict provision that it should be used only for hiring help to tend to the necessary chores in my garden. Anyone who says he actually likes weeding or mowing the yard either lies or has deficient powers to discriminate between what is irksome and what is pleasurable. In my garden, I have generally followed the path of least resistance—working with what I've got, rather than engaging in grand designs and then laboring long and hard to bring into being something that would be intentionally and perennially splendid, instead of just occasionally and accidentally fairly handsome.

Of course, the character of my garden is also determined by things beyond any human decision, mine or anyone else's. Geography and geology command that I must garden in sandy soil on terrain that is absolutely flat.

It's a lovely, almost perfect garden. But I can take no credit for it, for it isn't at all the product of imagination. It is a garden remembered, and like all memories, this one may not be exact in its details. There may have been no aconites.

It is   or was   Grace Root's garden, also known as the Root Glen. It was—or is—a real garden, in Clinton, New York, brought into being over many decades by Mrs. Root, the closest thing to a dowager empress I've ever known. I met Grace Root in 1967, when I moved with my family to a rented farm in Clinton, New York, having been chosen a charter member of the faculty of Kirkland College, the brand-new sister institution to Hamilton. Mrs. Root, a trustee, invited me for Sunday dinner. I declined, fearing that if I somehow displeased her—and she had a reputation for eccentricity—I would be out of a job. The next Sunday she again invited me and I again declined. The following Monday the president of Kirkland told me that I would again be invited to have dinner with Mrs. Root and warned me that *no one* turned her invitations down, certainly not three times running.

The next Sunday at noon, my wife and I arrived. My fears turned out to be groundless. Mrs. Root, who had moved out of the big white house after turning it over to Hamilton for an art center, greeted us warmly at the door of the rambling, one-story cottage formerly occupied by her head gardener. Although she was badly afflicted by arthritis and needed a cane to walk, she was lively in mind and spirit.

"Please sit here with me," she said. "I hear you are a gardener. Tell me, do you also like dry vermouth? If so, I think we shall get on very well indeed."

It was the first of many visits. We drank more dry vermouth than I like to confess—or than I found comfortable the next morning. She told me that she had been friends with Edmund Wilson, Dorothy Parker, and Alexander Woollcott, who is buried in the cemetery at Hamilton College. She talked about his funeral. Through some mistake, his body had been shipped not to Hamilton College in Clinton, New York, but to Colgate College in Hamilton, New York. It took hours to correct the error, and when the coffin was lowered, it slipped, splattering mud on the mourners, causing Dorothy Parker to remark, "How like him— throwing dirt until the very last." Somewhere in the middle of our fourth vermouth, Grace was no longer "Mrs. Root," and she was telling me about the time she and her late husband went to Turkey and collected wild tulip seeds for the Glen. She mentioned along the way that a preacher in Clinton had once denounced her as "the scarlet woman of College Hill," adding, "You cannot imagine what satisfaction I take in the fact that his church has now been turned into a town art center."

After dinner Grace Root invited us to survey the garden from the walled area at the top, as she told us its history. She mentioned that she feared that on her death Hamilton College would want to take it over and turn it into a ski slope.

"But that won't happen," she said. "I've spent a lifetime making this garden, and I've seen to it that my death won't be its undoing." She spoke of foundations, trusts, complicated legal strategies with only one purpose—the perpetual care and tending of her garden, which she had already opened to the public.

During my three years in Clinton, I visited her garden a great many times. There were other Sunday dinners and much more vermouth. We corresponded from time to time after I moved away, but her hand-writing grew increasingly faint and spidery. Then one day I heard that Grace Root had died in New York City, where she always spent her winters.

I trust that her legal strategies worked, that her garden is still there, as lovely as ever. If it isn't, I don't want to know.

A Garden
of Primroses

JOSEPHINE NUESE

HEN I am an old, old woman with long grey moustaches, a baggy tweed suit, stout boots and a cane, (what do you mean, when?) I shall have a whole garden of primroses. All kinds. Each growing in its preferred spot. For some primroses like wet feet and some do not, some like to grow in a gravelly bank, some like to nestle between rocks in a shadowy woodland, some like a touch of sun. Most of them want a deep, rich, humusy bedding a little on the acid side but some, like the *auriculas*, are happy only in lime-flavored gravel.

My primrose garden will be a swale of fairly open woodland with rocks, flickering sunlight, ferns, a spray of primrose-footed white birches at the far end against a great grey boulder . . . there will be a little stream where, along the damp sides, will be white, lavender, rosy-pink drifts of the very early primrose *P. denticulata* neighbored by small ferns whose fronds will unfurl later . . . further down the stream, edging out into the morning sun, will be groups of the taller and later *P. japonica* in white and deep pink . . . and all along these moist edges, spilling into the water, will be masses of the pale blue brook forget-me-nots *(Myosotis palustris)* to bloom from late spring all through the summer.

And there will be a little path, not even a path, just a way of going, meandering towards the stream and the half-glimpsed birches beyond. Here and there along this path, among rocks, will be occasional groups of simple native azaleas footed by clumps of the great-leafed Bergenia *(Saxifraga cordifolia)* which shelter carpets of the tiny *juliana* primroses—white, purple, apricot—and a good blue strain of *P. acaulis* merging, further back, into drifts of the white, cream, and pale yellow garden primrose *Polyanthus* set among ferns . . . this, in turn, lifting to a low bank of rocky, humusy limey gravel studded with the evergreen tufts of *auriculas*—yellow buff, pink, purple . . .

If you can take the above and still keep on reading, look up primroses *(Primulas)* in H. Lincoln Foster's *Rock Gardening* and glimpse the further and almost infinite variety of primroses which you can dream about as you become more experienced with these gentlest of all plants. The kinds listed above are among the easiest.

For, contrary to popular belief, most primroses are very easy to grow if you give them even a reasonable facsimile of the soil and site they want. There are, of course, difficult ones which will be a little querulous at times but most of them are remarkably sweet tempered. All of them are best bought from primrose specialists who offer not only the best plants but also the best colors, widest assortment of kinds to choose from.

They are also easy from seed. Some authorities recommend that you freeze the seed (just stick the seed pan in the freezing compartment of your ice box) and this is advisable if you are dealing with seed of uncertain age, but fresh seed, I am told by primrose growers, does not need this treatment.

But I know from my own experience how easy they are from seed, how loving and forgiving, for once I grew a panful which survived a

Jospehine Nuese

traumatic experience. I had frozen them as above, they had sprouted generously and, believing they liked cool temperatures, I had stuck them in the cold pantry for further growing. Shortly thereafter, through some accident, the cat got shut up in the cold pantry overnight and decided that the earth-filled pan was a new kind of sandbox. When I released him the next morning the tiny primroses had been scattered far and wide, most of them with their roots up. I fixed a new pan, stuck them into fresh soil, and they picked up right where they had left off. They are that easy.

Another delight in growing primroses from seed is that they often produce sports (i.e., mutations, variations in form, habit or color) which may turn out to be a primrose the likes of which no one has ever seen before. This is one of the most exciting experiences which can happen to a gardener and sets you up among the experts—in your own estimation anyhow—from which elevation you can afford to be gracious and a little condescending to other primrose growers. This does a lot for your morale if not for your popularity.

A garden of primroses is especially recommended for the elderly because it needs little care. The small plants are so light and so easy to handle, so easy to divide every few years, need so little attention, that most primrose-gardening can be done sitting down; all you need is a trowel and a low stool. There is none of the deep digging, hefting of large plants, which accompanies most other forms of gardening and, in the shaded area where most primroses like to grow, there are few weeds. Primroses are for those who, for one reason or another, have had to give up heavy gardening.

If you are in this category, consider primroses. Buy just a few to start with, then begin raising your own from seed, and before you know it you will be launched upon the primrose path which, as everyone will tell you, leads to the skids.

A Garden of
Paving Stones

VITA SACKVILLE-WEST

OW much I long sometimes for a courtyard flag-
ged with huge grey paving-stones. I dream of it at
night, and I think of it in the daytime, and I make
pictures in my mind, and I know with the reason-
able part of myself that never in this life shall I achieve such a thing, but
still I continue to envy the fortunate people who live in a stone country,
such as the Cotswolds, or in the northern counties of Yorkshire, West-
morland, and Cumberland. In this courtyard should grow all kinds of low
plants between the flags, encouraged to seed themselves freely . . . and
just as I had reached this point in my article the post arrived, with a letter
asking if I had ever seen a very small garden entirely paved and allowed
to become a rug of flowers?

No, I had not, but I had often thought of it, for it seemed a
solution to the recurrent problem of the pocket-handkerchief garden,
which is all that many people are now able to enjoy. It would be extremely
labour-saving: no mowing, no weeds. And very pretty and original. I
forsee two objections: the initial cost of the stones, and the fact that most

people do like a bit of green grass. There are, however, some elderly or handicapped people to whom the bit of green grass is more of a worry than a pleasure; and as for the cost of the stone, it is possible to use home-made cement blocks which are much cheaper and which in any case would soon get partially covered over. Lakes of aubretia, bumps of thrift, mattresses of yellow stone-crop, hassocks of pinks, rivulets of violets: you see the idea?

Amongst these essential and fundamental coverings I should plant small treasures. Shall we say as an axiom that a very small garden should have very small things in it? The picture should fit the frame. I should have lots of little bulbs, all the spring-flowering bulbs; then for the later months I should let the pale-blue Camassias grow up and some linarias, both pink and purple, such easy things, sowing themselves in every crevice. Every garden-maker should be an artist along his own lines. That is the only possible way to create a garden, irrespective of size or wealth. The tiniest garden is often the loveliest. Look at our cottage gardens, if you need to be convinced.

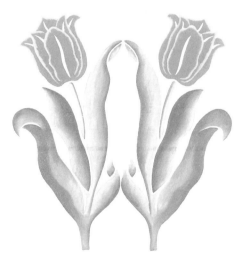

URING early boyhood, I paid long visits at the home of a dear old grandmother, in one of the most thoroughly crystallized towns of New England. Grandmother was a Quaker of the old school, and a pillar of the meeting, consequently everything about her was of the approved old-time sort. The garden, certainly, was no exception to the rule. I think I see now, the sober, dignified Quaker ladies, attired in suitable dove-color, pacing the garden walks or daintily plucking flowers. Surely finer flowers never grew than were reared in that garden, for the maintenance it received was exquisite. What sunny hours we children spent in it. And it was truly a charming spot, though something must be allowed for the glamour of boyish freshness and spirits. I feel, indeed, after seeing all the modern inventions, that I could cheerfully forego the most blazing effects that we behold nowadays on expensive lawns, for the privilege of enjoying once more the old garden behind grandmother's house. I wish you could see the quaint old place as I recall it after the lapse of many years. It was, I confess, a somewhat formal and prim affair; but there was nothing commonplace or

vulgar about it, as in the baser sort of what is now called ribbon gardening. On the contrary, there was a distinct flavor of individuality in the character of its appearance. The designer, being either a practical housewife, or inspired by one, had thought of many things besides mere ornament, and even the ornament had a distinct difference, which gave this garden a special suggestiveness of its own.

The paths were laid out with entire regularity, and marked with long rows or borders of dwarf box; but there the regularity and sameness ceased, unless we count as regular the scrupulously kept gravel of the walks, bedded with white pebbles. Such a garden naturally had its grape-vine, trained on some suitable supports, which, in this case, happened to be the stable wall. The next-door neighbor, I remember, had an arbor for his grape-vines, that began, as it seemed, nowhere in particular, and ended twenty feet off with the most delightful neglect of any why or wherefore, except that it existed for the grape-vine; that was evidently enough for Deacon Jones. Nowadays such an arbor must have done duty alike as a place for seats, for a promenade, and also for the display of architectural ornament in the Queen Anne style. Not that such a triple performance of duty is not proper enough, but only it was not the way of gardens of those earlier days.

For the economies of the house, there were all sorts of fragrant herbs, such as thyme, sweet-marjory, sage, mint, and half a dozen other sweet-smelling and savory plants, that were on this account, however, none the less attractive as ornaments of the garden. They were not only delightful in themselves, but delightful because they reminded us of grandmother's wonderful storecloset, from which issued so many good things.

But grandmother's garden was, before all things, a productive flower garden. Unlike modern gardens, created for external show alone, it was a real storehouse of color and odor, out of which one could, day after day, gather rich treasures, and yet leave its beauty apparently undimmed. Everybody about the house, boys included, was welcome to pluck a flower occasionally without let or hindrance. The flowers, indeed, seemed actually

to enjoy being plucked. They were not, of course, specially rare, and yet I am sorry to say that it might be difficult to find some of them nowadays. Their simple charms have, in fact, been almost entirely obscured by the glittering novelties of the modern horticultural world. For instance, there were those rich old damask roses. They are seldom if ever seen now; and yet what masses of them there were in grandmother's garden, and how well I remember their rich color, and the delightful odor they exhaled when the dew was resting on their petals. Where shall we find now such beds of sweet-scented pinks—not carnations, but real hardy pinks—and such sweet-williams? In few places; for they are out of fashion now. Tall clusters of phloxes stood here and there. Blue larkspurs, tall, quaint, and lovely, nodded above carpets of portulaca vine, studded with scarlet flowers. Broad patches of the gorgeous herbaceous peony were striking in effect, close by the straggling foliage and flowers of the sweet-pea. Great hollyhocks were there, too, with richly colored single petals, the pure outlines and decorative appearance of which fail not to charm the eye even now, amid the multitudinous resources of the modern gardener.

Snowdrops, crocuses, and other bulbs used to spring up as if by magic, year after year, in secluded spots of grandmother's garden. Evidently no definite arrangement had been applied to any of these plants, but somehow they were seen to be greatly to the advantage of the general effect. All stood together, just as they happened to come, behind the borders of box, in the rich, weedless brown earth. How fresh that brown earth smelled as it was dug up in early spring! Of other climbers than the grape-vine there were few. Wistarias, clematises, and the long list of similar plants of the present day were little used then. Filling their place in their own attractive way, were delicate morning-glories and graceful cypress vines, trained with some formality and with almost reverential care.

These reminiscences may and should have a distinct purpose and effect on present landscape gardening undertakings. Let our circumstances and intentions be what they may, we can certainly build up for ourselves once more some genuine development of these quaint old garden recollections. We can, I think, do it all the better if we are poor and have only a half acre or a scant 25 × 100-foot lot.

In that case we should make a pilgrimage to Sunnyside (Irvington, N.Y.), and see how Washington Irving did, by fine instinct alone, for he was hardly a landscape gardener, what few landscape gardeners would have the simple self-control to attempt. A plain rambling house set on the banks of the Hudson with one walk winding from the picturesque lane to the porch and door-step, half a dozen or more elms and maples, a few simple flowers, blue and white, along the base of the dwelling, and you have literally all there is of the lawn. Not a coleus bed, not a shrub, nothing but exquisitely kept turf and a few stately old trees. The repose, the dignity, the quaint simplicity, and unconscious self-restraint of Sunnyside is my ideal of what a small place should be with a grandmother's garden behind it.

But the reader will say, perhaps, I have my acres of land with drives, rhododendron groups, shrubberies, green houses, beds of cannas and coleuses, and yet why cannot I too have my grandmother's garden? You can have it, without doubt, but since it will be necessarily out of keeping with the general scope of your place, you will have to isolate it and shut it from view with large trees and shrubs, so that it will be a surprise when discovered, and not count in the general effect of the lawn.

In order to explain what I mean, I have introduced a plan of a place near Orange, N.J., where just this arrangement for a grandmother's garden was undertaken. It is not, of course, exactly what we remember our grandmother's garden to have been, *other times, other manners*—but it is built on the same plan, amplified and perfected in accordance with the richness of our modern list of perennial garden plants. It is less quaint, I acknowledge, less old-timy, but it has as much quaintness as the old rooms with the grandmother's furniture seen in modern houses, and is quite as much in keeping.

Let us look at the plan. It represents a place of three acres. There is a broad drive that sweeps up to the front of the house and then turns and passes out to the barn. All along the sides of the place are planted continuous borders of mixed trees and shrubs intended to secure a sense of seclusion, while in front are left two openings to give a view of passers-by and a glimpse of outside life and companionship.

On the left of the house a walk winds from the front door to a fine old shade tree with a seat around it, and so along the outside border of shrubbery to a summer-house in the rear. At the back of the house the ground originally sloped up rapidly so that it became necessary to form a terrace in order to manage the drainage successfully.

Between this terrace and the house, shut in by shrubbery on both sides, was arranged a mat of carpet bedding carefully designed with *Alternantheras, Echeverias, Pyrethrums,* and *Gnaphaliums,* so as to secure an artistic arrangement of vivid green, yellow, red, and white. The spot is isolated, and part, as it were, of the architecture of the house. In such places only, on country places, do we consider planting of this kind admissible. In any other spot, away from the house, such designs are artificial and out of key.

Passing up two flights of stone steps that ascend to the terrace with their intervening terrace walk, we come to the terrace garden, or to what comes as near to the grandmother's garden as we ought to expect to get on such a place.

It consists of a plat of green turf with the corners cut to an octagonal line, and then a border of eight feet for the regular hardy garden flowering plants, lined on the farther side by clipped walls of California privet.

On either corner of the grass plat are tall urns for flowers, and still farther in are tall clusters of grasses, making four keypoints of effect. One of these is made of the dazzling white variegated bamboo *(Arundo Donax variegata)*, sometimes called ribbon grass, mingled with a blazing spike or two of the red-hot poker plant or *Kniphofia alceoides (Tritoma Uvaria grandiflora)*. These plants are not entirely hardy, and need protection in a cellar during winter. Another of these groups is made up of a tender but splendid-looking grass, *Gynerium argenteum*, pampas grass, with graceful foliage and long silvery plumes. The third clump consists of the hardy *Erianthus Ravennae*, resembling pampas grass, and growing ten or twelve feet high. *Eulalia Japonica variegata* and *zebrina* constitute the fourth and best clump. They are entirely hardy and very ornamental with their leaves striped and banded with white, and their stalks four to six feet high, bearing curly-feathered plumes. *Festuca glauca* and *Stipa pennata* have also their places as attractive grasses.

And now we may indicate the special points of resemblance in this design to the grandmother's garden. They are to be found principally in the border of plants eight feet wide that skirts the walk and grass plat. Each angle of this grass plat is cut off, making a large eight-sided figure with four long and four short sides. A strip of turf two feet wide is first left, and then comes the mixed skirting border of hardy perennial plants, relieved against the dark green clipped wall of privet. Here, as in the grandmother's garden, there is plenty of color and odor scattered about in somewhat promiscuous fashion, and ready to the hand for plucking or not, as the passing mood may determine.

In a general way, the large-growing plants are placed at the back, beyond a row of lower habit, and next the path we find the smaller specimens. Taken as a whole, however, the appearance of the plants, one to two feet apart, would be called entirely irregular, and instead of bare spaded earth, generally considered necessary in such places, the entire surface beneath the plants is covered with varieties of hardy creepers, such as moneywort, periwinkle, sedum, sandwort, mountain everlasting, arabis, or rock cress, not forgetting the pretty creeping forget-me-not, and the turfing daisy, with its lovely little flowers.

All the plants in this border are entirely hardy, and will last for many years without being renewed. Any one may enjoy here abundant color and odor of the most charming kind, for the greater part of the year. First, in early spring, peep out flowers of the lovely blue hepaticas, of the trailing arbutus, the dainty New England mayflower, and certain of the anemones or wind-flowers. The bloodroot, *(Sanguinaria Canadensis)* too, very dwarf, is always eagerly looked for in early spring, on account of the delicate charm of its pure white buds tenderly enfolded with leaves; later on, a clump of its opened flowers are very showy.

Then in May come still more, and, if possible, lovelier flowers, many of which last on far into summer. Such are larkspurs, garden pinks, the exquisite stemless gentian *(Gentiana acaulis)*, candy tuft *(Iberis)*, the asphodels, favorites of the ancients; several beautiful species of violets, and charming species of anemone, still blooming on into summer. Strictly summer-blooming kinds of herbaceous plants there are, of course. Here, in summer, are bright yellow *Achilleas*, the quaint and exquisite blue and yellow *Aquilegias*, or hardy columbines, with strangely formed petals, the dainty harebells, showy *Coreopsises*, day lilies, certain lovely species of gentian, the wonderful scarlet cardinal-flower, brilliant red poppies, rich blue and scarlet foxglove like *Pentstemons*, *Veronicas*, white *Astilbe Japonica*, the garden phloxes, *Liatris* or blazing star, and the purple foxglove.

Autumn flowers are not forgotten. Masses of goldenrod *(Solidago)*, and orange-colored milkweed *(Asclepias)*, and purple asters are scattered throughout the border; the blue *Aconitum autumnale*, or autumn monk's-hood, the curious chelone, or turtle's head, and the dwarfer kinds of sunflowers.

Last, but not least, just before winter sets in, we dwell with delight on the brilliant yellow and purple flowers of the chrysanthemums and Christmas roses. Your attention has been directed in this description to only a few of the plants in this border of mixed hardy flowers. More than a hundred and fifty varieties are used.

Before leaving the subject, it seems worth while to dwell for a moment on the Japan irises, planted in distinct lines within three formal recesses of the California privet, arranged for their reception. They appear in the spring, and present, with their curious forms and hues—as strange and beautiful in their way as any orchid—one of the most unique and charming effects in the entire garden. The broad, straight paths that run past all these flowers, and the grass plat and croquet ground make a worthy frame for our border, and everywhere the eye meets, at almost any season of the year, objects of interest.

This place has, therefore, an attraction that is related somewhat to the charm grandmother's garden possessed for us in early days. There is, first, the neatness and perfect keeping that suits the level space adjoining a terrace and the architectural lines of a house, and then there is all the profusion, and far more than the variety, that characterized the floral treasures of the old-fashioned example. More than that, we have individuality of beauty, which is, in one sense, the best of all beauty, fostered in the highest degree. One's economical instincts are satisfied with the idea of possessing flowers that need no re-setting year by year, and one's instinct for beauty can certainly ask for no more abundant feast than is here spread out.

If I Were Beginning Again

MARION CRAN

ORE than thirty years ago I stood upon a sharp hillside looking bewildered upon some three acres or so of ragged scrub flanked with pine and bracken. It was dull and untidy. The idea of a "garden" was suggested to me.

As set forth in "The Garden of Ignorance," I approached what in the end was to become the master passion of life in a most airy not to say flimsy way. I knew nothing; radio did not exist, nor did the daily Press instruct the amateur from week to week with "now is the time to." Everything had to be discovered from the ground upwards; people today are taught; I had to *learn*.

Breathless delight and enthusiasm, strength and energy hand in hand with the blackest ignorance made in the end my garden there; a charming place too, but not nearly as wonderful as it would be now if Time would turn back and I might begin again.

Alas! the tumbling years!

To learn by mistakes in the garden is a very long affair; impatient youth has to wait on Nature's measured rhythm and work in tune with the inexorable pulse of the seasons.

Hot rages of disappointment; impotent flurries of disgust; cowardly retreats behind the bad gardener's smoke screen—"Mine is such awful soil."

Here and there unexpected accidents of success. And at last I began to watch and to listen.

It was not mine, I found, to coerce and to dictate; if I wanted to have a happy garden, I must ally myself with my soil; study and help it to the utmost, untiringly. And then on top of that I must plant only those things which prefer the soil of that garden, a light, sandy medium on a waterless and arid hill; I must avoid any that need heavy, damp, and luscious clay.

Always the soil must come first. Before any ignorant preferences for show roses, tall trees of oak and ash, rich deep lawns, grass orchards thick with daffodil and primrose, and other delights of heavy land.

After fifteen years on hungry sand, just as I was beginning to learn its lesson, Life changed its shape, it tossed me out of Surrey across to the deep buttery clay of the Kentish weald, to Coggers where I made another garden.

But often, in the quiet hours of reflection that come with years and solitude, I go back in fancy to that first sandy garden and make pictures of what it would be like if I were beginning again.

Money that went to expensive failures would now go into improving the soil; that thirsty, lean, unloving stuff would be reinforced with all the clay possible to import into it; it should become kind; adhesive to the touch; retentive.

A queer thing about digging clay into sand, by the way, is that it *stays!* Twenty years after (and for all I know for ever) one may pick up a handful of sandy soil so treated and squeeze it to find it still has body, is still retentive. It does not run through the fingers like the sand through an hour-glass, as once it did.

Unfortunately, the reverse is not true; sand dug into clay does not remain to aerate the slippery stuff. Clay seems just to devour sand as the Goodwin Sands devour ships! Odd. But there it is.

The sand then, having by clay importations got some guts, I should profitably feed it thereafter with turfy loam, leaf-mould, farmyard manure; with beautiful composts rotted down by the Rudolf Steiner anthroposophical methods to supply humus; with pleasant stimulants of bonemeal and basic slag in their seasons.

If by any means feasible water should be secured on that hot hillside garden, to keep it cool and green in scorching summer weather; a runnel, a spraying fountain, a stream. One can grow practically anything on sand (aye, even on an ash heap) if there is a consistent water supply, as all desert dwellers know.

And then in this garden to which I go in dreams "beginning again" with all the energy of youth and the knowledge of age, I should plant the beautiful things which are happy in light warm soil. Not cram Dame Edith Helen, Queen of Spain, and vigorous Hybrid-Musks into dry sand without a spoonful of food or drink to stay their starving deaths, as once.

But instead I would turn to the rose species: Hugonis, the early primrose yellow, its bloom delicious against the feathery grace and fair spring green of a background of birches in various lovely forms, the weeping one (betula pendula Youngii), the cut-leaf (B. laciniata), our native silver birch "the lady of the woods" (B. verrucosa), the dark satin shining bark of betula nigra. And of course betula tristis!

In sheltered places yellow Banksia roses are happy on warm soil; one could plant them and that continuous bloomer, Phyllis Bide, to run her long canes up into overhanging boughs.

Roses too with the Persian Yellow ancestry which often makes for delicacy of constitution in colder soils; the dainty China roses, and the Noisettes, *not* forgetting Mme. Alfred Carrière, who flourishes even under tropic rays given ample rains.

The Ayrshire roses and the Bourbon (notably Coupe d'Hébé and Zéphyrine Drouhin); Farrer's pretty "threepenny bit" rose, rubrifolia with its attractive unusual foliage and handsome fruits; sericea pteracantha, the species with large blood-red thorns shaped like a tiger's tooth and just as big. One grows it only for those thorns, strange and spectacular as ruby glass when the sun shines through them.

Another rose species I would not forget, the one which adores a warm south wall on hot light soil, rosa sinica anemone. It spreads far and wide carrying a profusion of large fragrant pink saucers like enormous wild roses, in May and June.

Then masses of Michaelmas daisies for "awe-time," (as the soldier-sculptor called autumn), ranging from early-flowering alpines to the new dwarf hybrids, nine inches high; and then through the decorative shades of aster amellus to the splendid bushes of novae angliae and novi belgii, in all colours from snow white to richest red, blue, and purple, and in all heights from three to five feet.

Brooms in every colour, heathers and heaths in every form, azaleas in massed colour and fragrance lovely beyond belief, and rhododendrons on the acid Surrey sand.

No oaks in that garden but resinous, murmuring pines in plenty carpeted with blacken; and snowdrifts of amelanchier canadensis to change later in the year to glorious foliage colours. They call this small shapely tree Snowy mespilus in Surrey and under the boughs I have watched at nights in long-ago summer evenings night-jars make their strange soundless aerial dance.

All these things grow happily and others naturalise and make sweet spreads of colour in that kind of soil; muscari for instance and crocuses in variety; under the bracken-sheets lilies of the valley will be content increasing year by year.

They do not mind the pines or the fern roots and they adore the shade of bracken which keeps them cool when their bloom-time is over.

It is a perfect combination. By the way, the fragrant lilies of the valley will amply reward a yearly offering, in February, of good well-rotted farmyard manure.

Pines are commonly supposed to be "poisonous" to all delicate flower growth, because of the turpentine in the carpet of needles underneath them. One often hears "nothing will grow under pines." Yet here is an exception well worth proving.

So many herbs are sweeter, finer in flavour and in the fragrance of their essential oils when grown on well-worked sand, that a really nice herb garden is one of the features to make without any delay; chervil, *true* tarragon (hard to get!), all the thymes and savouries, sweet basil, chives, carraway, lavender, rosemary, and many another housewife's delight.

One of these is that most delicious herb fennel. It does not seem to enjoy the popularity it deserves. The delicate feathery foliage is very excellent chopped like parsley and put in "melted butter" sauce to serve with salmon and mackerel, but the best part of fennel is the root. Where the stems fold over just under the ground they thicken into a nice fat lump. This, cooked in boiling salted water, strained and then served whole with some fresh butter dabbed on, makes a dish to remember; it has something of the look of celery, not much, but a distant likeness; and it has a distinct taste of aniseed in the sweetness and freshness of the cooked vegetable. Those who "take to it," as they say, are liable to pursue it with a passion, as do enthusiasts for caviare, oysters, asparagus, seakale, and the like. Fennel root is certainly a delicious vegetable for those of selective taste.

I always imagine that I am "beginning again" in the same spot on Surrey sand as that on which I, a sophisticate, first touched the mysteries of earth and fell headlong into an enchantment from which I have never recovered.

Or ever will! Nature with her wonders blinds and binds one still. There is no escape. I love her utterly through all time and times.

All over the world towns to me are prison; green fields are home.

Yet if I might choose I should like to have different soil and make a garden on chalk. When I make this remark to friends they are upset. "But you will not be able to grow rhododendrons or azaleas, primulas or blue poppies. You will miss so many glorious things!"

What do I care? I am englutted of these fat rhododendrons and acid-loving plants. On chalk I can have other things, pinks in fragrant masses and fascinating colours, shirley poppies, far more exciting than the coddled blue ones in their soggy peaty stations, brave and varied hosts of other poppies, too, are at home on chalk.

Then there are clematis, wallflowers, madonna lilies, crown imperials, cherry trees (*all* the cherries!), pasque-flowers, cowslips, lilacs, forsythia, mock-orange, peonies, gypsophila, and many many shrubs. Scores of the things which I do long to grow at their best, would flourish in a limey place; perhaps a gritty limestone would do almost as well, but deep in my bones is a hankering for tiresome amusing chalk!

Once more, profiting by the lessons of the "garden of ignorance," I would first work the soil. That is the supreme lesson of the years. Humus is necessary on chalk; in every possible way and form; humus, even to shoddy when planting trees and shrubs.

To heavy sticky clay one gives air . . . deep digging, plenty of lime, ashes and "dentures," as they call burnt earth in Kent, dug in to loosen and aerate; and likewise drainage. That is most important. "Drainage for heavy soil!" If one wants to learn about that one should talk to Bob Pringle or Sandy Prain. Those two Scots are experts on draining soggy land; they *know!* Arid hungry sand must be enriched, made retentive, given heart.

"If I were beginning again!"

Does one get a chance in the Life that Alice knows now, to profit by the mistakes made in this?

So many of our lessons are learned, it would seem, too late to use on Earth.

My Garden

RUSSELL PAGE

 HIS book could have been called *Other People's Gardens* if this title had not been used already. I have no garden of my own and what I have learned has been from the years of working on other people's ground. But I allow myself day-dreams that I one day mean to have.

I hope that it will be on land which is neither chalky nor too acid, with soil to which I can add peat or lime. I hope, too, for soil which is not heavy clay that takes years of back-breaking labour to lighten, nor a hot dry sand whose thirst for water and manure I could never assuage.

It must be a small garden and a simple one; one man's work, mine perhaps, and in any case not so large as to need an armoury of mechanical devices or a full-time mechanic to keep these in running order. However good the soil, the first thing I shall do will be to make two enclosures, for compost, each five feet wide by ten feet long and walled in to a height of three feet. Into these will go everything that in a few months will ensure me a regular supply of rich black humus, since I know no better way of having a garden relatively free from pests and diseases. There are limits to the time, trouble and money I am prepared to spend on spraying my garden with chemical preparations which can so easily destroy nature's subtle balances and, by eliminating one pest, fatally leave the door open for others.

Once I have made this, the garden's future larder, I can start to consider the site. First of all I should say that I plan to make my garden in England since, all things considered, I do not know a better country. I would rather start with an old garden, however badly arranged and however neglected, since a few mature trees, an old wall and even a few square yards of good soil will give me the advantage of a twenty year start, all the more so as I shall be so late a starter. First I shall take out all the rubbish, elder bushes, nettle beds and any trees which are ugly and misshapen or too crowded. I shall thin out old shrubberies without pity and prune back any specimens which I may wish to keep and, later perhaps, transplant. All soft green rubbish will go to the compost heaps, the rest I shall burn and save the wood ash where I can. Only when I have cleaned the garden and ridded it of everything I know I will not want, shall I make a careful survey on paper as a basis for an eventual plan.

My garden will be very simple. There will be no herbaceous borders, no rose garden and no complicated formal layout with all the bedding out, edge trimming and staking which these forms of gardening involve. A ground-floor room in the house or a converted outbuilding will be my workroom, part library for garden books and catalogues, part studio for drawing board and painting materials, part tool shed for all the small tools, string, raffia, tins of saved seed and all the odd extensions and aids to the gardener's two hands.

I see my workroom with one wall all window, and below it a wide work table running its whole length with a place to draw and a place to write. Walls will be whitewashed, the floor of brick, there will be a fireplace and chairs for talk, and at least one wall lined with books.

This room will open south or westwards on to my working garden and I shall design this just like one of those black-japanned tin boxes of water-colours. I see this working garden as a rectangular space as large as I can afford and manage. With luck or good management or both, high walls will protect it to east and north and I shall enclose the other two sides with a low wall or a five feet yew or box hedge. Under the walls I shall make a three or four feet wide bed for climbing plants and others which like the warmth and shelter that a wall at their back will give them. I shall then divide the rest into small beds, perhaps four and a half feet or five feet square, separated by eighteen inch paths of bricks on edge or stone or even pre-cast cement flags of a good texture and colour and set, like the bricks or stone, in a weak cement mixture so that no weeds can grow. The number of beds and their exact dimensions will depend on the area of my ground but they must be small enough to be easily accessible from the paths surrounding them. In working out my simple criss-cross pattern I shall surely find it useful to have a few beds as double units, nine feet by four foot six or ten feet by five feet. In fact this garden will closely resemble the "system garden" of an old botanical garden whose small beds are each devoted to growing numbers of the different plant families. I shall use this garden as paint box, palette and canvas, and in it I shall try out plants for their flower colour, texture of foliage and habit of growth. In some beds I shall set out seedlings for selection, in others bulbs, in others plants combined for essays in colour. Each bed will be autonomous, its own small world in which plants will grow to teach me more about their aesthetic possibilities and their cultural likes and dislikes. I shall make no attempt at a general effect, for this will be my personal vegetable museum, my art gallery of natural forms, a trial ground from which I will always learn. I may use a flowering tree here or there above some of my postage-stamp squares in places where I want to grow plants which appreciate a dappled shade, and I may hollow out a square or two as pools for water lilies or *Iris kaempferi*.

So, close to my workroom, I shall have my palette, changing from year to year and season to season and accessible and workable in any weather. I see already a square with tufts of white and coral-feathered, scarlet and rose-pink tulips whose foliage as it dies off will be covered by the new leaves, blue-grey, green or yellow-green striped with white, of the various hostas, and camassias with their sober flowers of lavender grey. In another square will grow *Euphorbia wulfenii* and hellebores and perhaps some long spurred aquilegias. There will be lilies too and lavender, some of the old-fashioned roses and all the garden pinks I can find. Perhaps I shall have a square or two of delphiniums, plants I like only in an enclosed garden. Here I shall test kurume azaleas for their colours as seen in sun or shade; primula species, rodgersias, moraeas and meconopses will grow in squares of specially moist and peaty soil, helianthemums and cistus in others which are sandy and dry. Here, I shall find, living and growing, the coloured expansions of my pleasures as a painter and gardener, as well as an addict of catalogues and dictionaries.

Only in an enclosed garden would I want to grow plants in this apparently chaotic way. Even so, any elaborate design, with axes and central features and with differing proportions of beds and paths of grass and water, would destroy the charm and defeat the purpose and meaning of this garden. This is why I shall make my plan a repetition of small units so that it will resemble the neatly partitioned drawers of a numismatist's cabinet or more exactly, a page from a stamp collector's album.

I do not find it easy to envisage my future garden without its house—it is like drawing a body without a head. But whether the house is large or small, its walls will be covered with climbing plants and below them there will be growing things. Against the house, in full sun and sheltered from the wind, there will be a wide paved space and perhaps to one side a few rectangular flower beds edged with box or lavender. I am a tulip addict and will not be able to deny myself a bed or two of tulips and pansies, forget-me-nots, wallflowers and bachelor's buttons in spring. In summer I shall plant these beds with thick patches of half-hardy annuals. Only a prophet can know which to plant each year. In a wet summer zinnias will be a failure, (and I love white zinnias and white tobacco flowers near a house); or I shall try a particoloured bed of *Phlox drummondii* only to see them wither to nothing in a scorching season. But I am willing to try my luck rather than forgo petunias and fuchsias, ageratums, dwarf dahlias, hardy chrysanthemums—all gaudy flowers whose place is near the house.

As with the house, I cannot predict my future landscape. I should like a stream, and a fast running one too, at least for part of its course through the garden. If it drops in level three or more feet, I shall arrange to dam it in three or four places with stones artfully placed to give each little fall of water a different note, for one of my greatest pleasures is the sound of falling water. I would do little more by way of water gardening, as I do not care much for bog and waterside gardening in places where I can dispense with it. If the yellow flag iris grows there, and meadowsweet, perhaps I would replace the wild iris with the blues and whites of *Iris sibirica* and *Iris laevigata*, but discreetly and with a light hand; and if there were room I would add a few of the tall pink herbaceous *Spiraea venusta*. I should certainly try to establish *Primula rosea* along the moist part of the stream's banks because of a predilection for the bright carmine pink of this Himalayan plant, so unusual a colour in early April. In the showers and fleeting sunshine of early spring, *Primula rosea* looks as stalwart and happy as a native primrose, so vigorous and strong and so prolific that it ought, years since, to have naturalised itself down half a hundred English streams. As far as I know it never has, but I shall be satisfied to go on trying to encourage it. I may, too, allow myself a clump or two of *Primula florindae*. I know it is coarse compared with the lovelier *P. sikkimensis*, but, coming in July, its tall heads of drooping cowslip yellow flowers look native and it establishes itself easily. So much for my stream. I hope it will be shaded along its course just for the faint mystery it evokes as it emerges from shadow into sunlight and for this I may want to aid and plant a simple native tree or two.

The main part of my garden will take the shape of a pool of lawn, which may run level away from the house or perhaps rise or fall. It may extend from the house thirty yards or sixty or a hundred, but whether it is wide or long, whether it runs up hill or down, I shall try to give it a shape complete in itself. It will be the vital open space which links and gives meaning to everything else—house and hedges, trees and plantings, the clear or cloudy sky. To enhance them all I shall try to give this open space a definite but not rigid form. As I do not see the house as an architectural gem demanding a formal treatment, I shall avoid a formal shape and define it nearest the house with curving hedges or some simple and unified planting scheme. Farther away I shall try to outline its shape

by light and shade, rather than underline it by a rigid and brightly coloured planting. I shall think of this, the centre of my composition, as an enclosure rather than as a glade. Glades, at least as they are used to-day, suggest a succession of irregular capes and bays with carefully planted groups of flowering shrubs. In a curious way these imply dispersion, a theme which best suits large properties where you are thus drawn farther and farther into the garden to discover new walks and vistas. But mine will be a small garden and my theme should suggest containment. If there is a view I will try to frame it in, so that it too contributes to the central open space which, for all its apparent emptiness, will still be a focus and centre. For here the vibrations, the intentions and qualities of all the different elements of the rest of the garden will meet and mingle to give the whole its unity.

Since I have chosen the English landscape as my setting, I shall avoid pushing any abstract forms too far. I would not try to merge house and garden in the Californian manner, as the climate will make this an uncomfortable anomaly, nor would I aim to embody the abstractions of my concept in a wilfully exotic way. The mood I seek above all is one of relaxation given by a garden, easy and untortured, in which plants, however rare and strange, will grow and take their place naturally and discreetly.

In the back of my mind lurks the picture of some native growth of trees, a few beech or oaks or birch perhaps or Scots fir, some form of little copse with hazel stools or a few wild hollies. Or if this is an old garden there may be a few good trees or an overgrown orchard, so that some good part of my garden has a canopy of leaves and the silhouettes of trees to break the skyline. If there are spruce and fir, out they will come: most small gardens are better without them. I might spare a fine isolated horse-chestnut or sycamore but I should remove both at once if they were in any place which I intended to plant: the chestnuts because they make a dank and sour shade in which even ivy can scarcely grow and the sycamores for their graceless youth and their unlovely foliage, usually blackened with disease by July. Canadian poplars would share the same fate.

Perhaps my main grass area will reach as far as the foot of the nearest trees. If so, I will define its edge by fairly compact drifts of large shrubs chosen for their effectiveness as mass and texture rather than for the colour of their flowers. These might be box or yew or perhaps rhododendrons or viburnums or cotoneasters. As they will mark the far limits of the lawn, I would not have them too brightly coloured. The scarlet or strong rose pink of certain rhododendrons, for instance, would falsify the whole perspective. Whether in the open or in shade, I would frame my lawn with carefully modulated greens and use clear pale colours—cream, pale yellows, soft pinks and blue mauves in sunshine and much white with clear mauve and accents of coral pink in the half light and shadows. I like white flowers, especially camellias, roses, rhododendrons, viburnums and hydrangeas, the silky whites of *Romneya coulteri*, the mauvy white satin of wood anemones and philadelphus "Belle Etoile," the icy snow-white of certain camellias and of the double white rugosa rose. By juxtaposition you can underline and bring out these different tonalities of white or enhance them by contrast and reflection.

I shall have to work warily with flower colour in such a small garden and avoid all the sensational and too dramatic effects of brilliant colouring, unless there is enough room to hide an occasional explosion of colour—reds and salmons and scarlets, black purple and orange—in places where they would not disrupt the pervading quiet harmony.

But the garden's most usual livery is, after all, green and I shall make it my main task to handle my plants and arrange them in their own terms of green. If I can succeed in groupings good in their form, textures and differing tonalities, I shall be sure of harmony throughout the yearly rhythm of the garden. Then only I will consider flower colour as an added study and delight.

At this point I have to warn myself quickly against the anaemic approach of certain modern purists who have pushed the theory of understatement in planting to ridiculous lengths, planting one bulrush and one *Caltha palustris*, for example, in a formal pool in the patio of some elaborate modern house, or else thinking that a patch of marram grass and a few tufts of osier will enhance the bright *avant-garde* conceits of a pavilion at an exhibition. Such aridities, and they are increasingly frequent, are a bleak denial of all the pleasures of gardening.

If I am prejudiced I am also tolerant and ready to understand a garden designer's revolt against the popular passion for bright flower colour at all costs. I remember a vast fan design of beds, a hundred square yards perhaps, solid with scarlet salvias spilling out over a rough grass slope in a public park in Geneva—a vulgar and thoughtless splash of colour, all the more surprising as it lies within a few yards of one of Europe's better rose gardens. At the other end of the same scale I think of a small English inland garden, often cited as a model of good planting and planning. Here under a grey and clouded sky I saw flower borders planted with infinite love and trouble in a most carefully thought-out scheme of purple and crimson and orange. Purple berberis and rhus, cascades of *Clematis jackmanii*, groups of *Phlox paniculata* in Tyrian purples and royal crimsons and well grown clumps of tiger lilies all combined to create a garden picture as strident as it was oddly funereal.

Between these two extremes of under and over-statement we have to tread carefully. I see my green lawn and its surroundings as the one part of my garden which I shall design entirely as scenery. Large or small, this link between the house and its surroundings will be an exercise in landscape composition.

I should like to keep my pool of lawn, and the planting which rings it, free from the hard intrusion of a path. I would rather make a path as an outer ring lying well behind the plantings that fringe and shape the lawn, and as a main line of communication linking all the parts of the garden. It will start somewhat formally, passing to one side of the house between flower beds. Here it may be of brick or stone, but as it passes round and through each part of the garden its material will change accordingly. To make sure that it dries quickly and is practicable in all weathers, I will give it a foundation of at least nine inches of broken stones or brick rubble and three inches of ashes or coarse gravel above that. Only then will I surface it with good binding sand and perhaps fine sieved and washed pea-gravel. Pea-gravel is better than crushed gravel or stone whose sharp edges will ruin even the stoutest shoes.

The path will make its way from the slightly formal arrangement of flower beds next the house through a series of secondary garden pictures, all lying outside and invisible from the central part of the garden. These will be as elaborate or simple as the nature of the garden and my own possibilities allow. Perhaps I shall be able to bring my path through plantings of flowering shrubs, large enough, maybe, to need narrow paths breaking away from the main one to rejoin it later. Here I would use sub-shrubs that I like and could make grow to break the edges of the paths— lavenders and potentillas, ceratostigma and caryopteris, leonotis and phlomis, cistus and helianthemum, and heaths, not all, nor all together, for my choice will depend on soil and site. I see all this as garden-planting, grouped harmoniously surely, but intimate and designed as garden and not as landscape. These small shrubs will be like foothills for the higher mounds of all the larger shrubs I might want to grow informally. I say informally as, if I have room, the lilacs and philadelphus, laburnums and other domesticated flowering shrubs will need another and slightly more formal setting in an enclosure which would include such roses too as I might want to grow. These are the roses which may be left to grow into large bushes with only an occasional pruning to remove dead wood and keep them in shape. I have a catholic taste and would happily mix the stronger-growing floribunda types, "Queen Eliza-beth" for instance, with shrub roses like "Fruhlingsgold," *R. nevada, R. gallica versicolor* as well as damask roses and *R. centifolia* and the lovely free-flowering perpetuals like "General MacArthur," "Ulrich Brunner" and "Caroline Testout." Nor would I leave out hybrid musk roses, such as "Penelope" and "Pax." In this part of the garden I see, amongst the bushy roses, thick clumps of perennials, too coarse-growing for my "system" garden, but which I would not like to be without: herbaceous paeonies and thalictrums and a dozen varieties of *Phlox paniculata* for their fresh colours and the honey sweetness they bring in late summer and all the Japanese anemones I could lay hands on. I would have crown imperials and *Galtonia candicans, Lilium candidum* and deeply planted clumps of certain tulips, cottage and Rembrandt, left in place to come up each year. In this way, although the individual flowers will be smaller, the clumps will increase and make great bouquets growing larger every year. Between all these will run my path primly bordered with London Pride or alchemilla or with the handsome foliage of bergenia or hostas.

At this point in our imaginary walk we might pause and consider the question of the kitchen garden. I have to think of it as a luxury—it would be my modest equivalent of the rich man's yacht or racing stable. I would want its produce but not at the cost of working it myself. But for the moment I will imagine myself with a neat kitchen garden divided by the path into four quarters, all neatly edged with box. For all it harbours slugs, needs cutting and is, in general, the working gardener's bane, I would not care for a kitchen garden without box edges and, as well, neatly pruned espaliers and cordons of apples and pears. In my four quarters I will grow only those vegetables whose taste is ruined if more than an hour elapses between their being culled and cooked—like asparagus, green peas, new potatoes and baby carrots. If ever I have this kitchen garden I shall make it an even costlier adventure by making all the paths in asphalt with gravel rolled into the final coat of bitumen or, of well-roughened concrete with wooden laths set in flush every three feet as expansion joints and to prevent crazing. Weeding paths is an appalling waste of time and the use of weedkillers means the death of anything growing along the edges.

chatter of broken and falling water. For these I will clear and dig a space large enough to hold a hundred plants in the hope that they will thrive and naturalise themselves: if they do not I shall not insist. *Salvia superba*, the purple meadow sage, is another wild plant I should like to grow among the meadow grasses as naturally as it does, along with the yellow tansy and milky-blue chicory, on the open roadsides of the Ile de France.

By now I have hopefully pictured an ambitious garden but one still without a small greenhouse where I could grow plants from seeds and cuttings and winter geraniums and fuchsias and other potted plants. I like pot gardening and would use plants in pots on steps, low walls and on my paved terrace space, grouping them in simple flower pots of all sizes. I should use cannas and yuccas and hedychium, *Francoa ramosa*, tigridias, yellow and white lantanas clipped into balls, and the dwarf pomegranate, which grows so easily from seed and whose neat foliage and flowers are an exact miniature of the ordinary orange scarlet pomegranate.

Part of the greenhouse I shall save for the pale blue *Plumbago capensis* and especially for *Jasminum polyanthum* so that through the winter months I can cut sprays of its brown-red buds and intensely fragrant white flowers. I shall have to find room too for bowls and dishes set with bulbs of narcissus "Paper White" to bring into the house for Christmas, for a few Roman hyacinths and scented creamy freesias and other spring flowers; there would always be enough for one small vase to relieve the dark days of winter. If I have two heated frames next to the greenhouse they will be enough to grow half-hardy annuals for my flower beds in good time for me to set out sturdy plants towards the third week in May.

Wherever I make my garden the main elements will not change: in front of the house a deliberately composed "landscape," so quietly arranged that one would not tire of it; nearby a working garden; and subsidiary to both of these, such additional features as the landscape, the soil and the site would indicate and as I could afford. To try and describe the structure of a nonexistent garden is, I fear, but to make a rusty catalogue. Walls, paths, trees, shrubs, lawns and terraces, lists of plant names, tool sheds, greenhouse, parking space and all the rest are like the separate pieces in a box of toys to be put together to make the structure and fabric of a garden. If that were all, it would be a slow and arid process, the mere application of technique and experience towards changing the external appearance of one tiny plot of ground—an infinitesimal point on the planet's surface—a pastime like another, as constructive, no more nor less, as playing patience or doing jigsaw puzzles.

A garden really lives only insofar as it is an expression of faith, the embodiment of a hope and a song of praise. These are high-sounding words but wherever I set my aim, high or low, the achievement, by the very nature of things as they are, is bound to fall far short of them and a too modest aim may well result in an insignificant achievement. I use the word aim perhaps too loosely, for I will surely have many aims in connection with every garden I attempt; the first perhaps quite simply is to leave a place more beautiful than I find it. By itself this is a subjective aim, one for my personal satisfaction and related to my own inevitably subjective ideas about beauty. So, at once, I have to expand or add to my aim and endeavour to understand the point of view of others. Will my garden spell for them the message it has for me? So my aim widens to include some understanding of my fellows. Nor can that be all or enough. I have to understand too the nature of all the processes that will go to make the garden, the rhythm of activities and where in each process this rhythm checks and falters and can resume only with the application of a stimulus at an exact moment. These are the rhythms also of all human as well as all vegetable processes: men, like trees, can be moved at certain moments and not at others. I draw and draw, searching for a composition which will come right in its own time only, perhaps at once, perhaps after hours and days of work. Of course the answer is inherent in the problem, and I find the solution only as soon and as clearly as I see all or enough of the factors which compose the problem. So now my aim

includes my own necessity for clearer thinking. You see now to where this leads, for a finer quality of thinking comes only with a wiser heart and where must I look to find the heart's wisdom? All these I must remember as I struggle with problems of drawing and composing on paper, with the spadework of calculations and lists, the difficulties of construction, the chance vagaries of behaviour of plants and men, soil and weather for which I have to remember to make allowances.

I am forced to a life-long discipline and a necessary and constant awareness so that eagerness may not turn into ill-temper and hopes not well based on facts founder in useless despair or wither into a frivolous cynicism.

When I come to build my own garden it can scarcely take another form than the one which is a reflection of its maker. If I want it to be "ideal," then I too must set myself my own ideal, my own aim. Now, as for a painter or a sculptor or any artist comes the test—what values does the garden-maker try to express? It seems to me that to some extent he has the choice. He may choose the easy way and design a garden as a demonstration of his technical skill and brilliance, go all out for strong effects or see the problem as one of good or bad business and so plan accordingly. Or he may try to make his garden as a symbol and set up as best he can a deliberate scaffolding or framework which nature will come to clothe with life. Perhaps circumstances will help him to decide that his garden theme should be devoted to water and so he will devote his garden to showing all the aspects he can of water: still and quiet water to reflect the soft green shade of summer trees, the purple greys of a coming storm or the brightness of white clouds crossing a clear blue sky, or shallow water running shining over a pebble bed or breaking into white foam where it falls. He may want to show water making lacy patterns against stone or bronze or use it in a hundred other ways to demonstrate its manifold aspects and attributes.

I can see another garden with another theme, one where the texture and shapes of foliage would be all important, a green garden which the eye would explore as it would an Altdorfer forest, layer upon layer of leaves sombre or caught in sunlight or in dappled silhouette. I remember a sequence in the Japanese film, "*Rashomon*," when the camera "travelled" with its lens focused upwards to the topmost branches of a forest set against the sky. As the endless succession of leafy patterns flickered across the screen, each with its definite shape and nature, one felt part of the world of trees and leaves and light and this, in quite another medium, gave to me at least a newly felt understanding of a whole dimension of the gardener's art.

In my garden I might choose to try and illuminate more especially one aspect of the force of nature. I could consider the growing point, the nose of a bulb of snowdrop or scilla and the strength and the heat it generates to force its way through the frozen earth, and then its symmetrical expansion of leaves and flower, in controlled and lovely explosion.

So often these and all the natural phenomena of spring pass unnoticed. We take them for granted and hardly look. Why should I not devise my garden deliberately as an act of appreciation to the forces which bring about this ardent growth? Why not design and plant some part of it to focus my attention and perhaps so widen my understanding of just this one aspect of nature?

After aconite and snowdrop the crocus next pierce through and then the early daffodils usher upwards all the spears of spring hyacinths and the orderly regiments of tulips. The fat buds of crown imperials come with the unfolding rosettes of *Lilium regale* and the deep red-brown knobs of paeonies which soon unfurl the elaborations of their young spring foliage. From the black mud burst the incredible spathes of *Lysichiton camtschat-cense* and arisaema and under the trees two more modest aroids, our native Lords and Ladies and the mousetail Arisarum pierce the woodland floor. Ferns no sooner break through the spring moist earth than the uncurled spring of each young frond uncoils with all the ogival curves and volutes of a Gothic crozier, and the blue-grey spear heads of flag iris burst from the ground sharp with the urgency of growth.

Those are the rites of spring, the earth turns and in a few sun-warmed hours the ice recedes and the soldanella's fringed lilac flower shines in a dark earth pocket against the snow.

My imaginary garden thus takes many forms and each of its forms has many aspects. Sometimes I see it as a sandy hollow ringed with dunes planted with marram grass against the shifting winds. Beyond the dunes the grey blue sea rolls and thunders on till the rhythm changes and it recedes leaving the long level reaches of sand glistening in the sun. My garden repeats in vegetable forms the shapes and colours of the waves with brakes of the silvery sea-buckthorn, *Hippophae rhamnoides*, and sea-green mounds of atriplex to protect wide plantings of blue-grey echinops and eryngium, static *Veronica hulkeana*, teucrium, silvery santolina and cistus and *Buddleia alternifolia*, senecios, *Cineraria maritima* and seakale;

all plants armoured in silver to meet the challenge of the sandy soil in this sunny and airy garden.

Like clouds moving across the sky dissolving and re-forming now in towering rounded masses, now in long streamers or curling wraiths, now jagged and torn or neatly spread in fish scale pattern over the sky, my garden's patterns shape and re-shape themselves. A leaf or a twig, the feel of a stone step under one's tread, a trickle of water, the musky smell of a cyclamen plant set in a pot that you have but to tap to know from the sound whether it needs watering or not, such transient impressions as these can open a door and set in motion a whole world of garden pictures. Each second is new and in each second are implicit a hundred gardens. In one it is sunset and suddenly there is a chattering in the pine trees and in the moment of evening's hush eight magpies wing through the air, drop down for a moment among the short grasses where the harebells flower and then, calling to each other, disperse and whirl severally back into the trees. Elsewhere the butterflies, peacocks and red admirals, settle thickly on the purple honey-scented panicles of buddleia. Below the great stone house is a lawn squarely hedged with dark green yew, where a white peacock spreads the splendour of his tail and sets his wing quills drumming. Where a russet brick bridge spans the moat, an old Persian lilac makes a mound of blossom to hang over the moss-green water where later the dragonflies will seem to tease the golden carp.

So, as in a kaleidoscope, the brightly coloured trifles shift and at each turn comes a new garden picture, dimensioned in time as well as space; where each leaf, though long since dead and withered, burgeons again and the gossamer web for ever catches the dew of a morning long since past.

Sometimes my garden seems like a mirage always receding but if ever this intermittent vision becomes a reality, wherever it is, whatever its size and shape it will be satisfying for like all gardens it will be a world for itself and for me.

A Garden
in the City

HENRY MITCHELL

BVIOUSLY if your garden is thirty-seven by ninety-six feet you deal with that space; if it is four and a half acres, you use your land differently. If a seventy-foot-high maple grows a few feet from your garden on a neighbor's land, clearly you make allowances for that disgusting fact. No garden exists apart from its setting—the particular climate of its geography, the nature of the soil, the presence or absence of large trees, walls, and existing plants. A gardener would not lightly saw down a thirty-foot-high box bush already growing in the garden he recently acquired, even if it is not where he would like it to be placed, or even if he did not particularly like box.

In short, and to save endless caveats, the reader is expected to know that no garden is "ideal" for all situations or for all gardeners. What follows is my own idea of a garden to suit myself and let us say it is a long narrow cat-run 40 by 185 feet in the nation's capital. The small house sits forty feet from the sidewalk in a neighborhood of large trees and neat lawns.

First, I would abolish the lawn, since the land in this small space forty feet square drops to sidewalk level in three terraces. And besides, I do not like lawns or the infernal racket of lawn mowers. Passing trucks and cars are of slight interest to me as well, and I would screen this fore-garden with a line of shrubs. A central walk would lead to the front door, and be given emphasis by an arch or small arbor at the sidewalk.

An endless variety of plants exists to glorify the entrance arch. In sun, few things excel a climbing rose, and my choice would be "Jaune Desprez," an everblooming creature introduced in 1832 and hardy at least to Philadelphia. The clustered blooms of pale apricot are two to four inches (depending on manure, water, and general care). The color is not strong at all, and sometimes it is mainly pink, sometimes yellow, and the musk fragrance is intense. This is a massive plant and would require heavy support.

In half-shade, where the rose would never be at its best, I would choose honeysuckles. Possibly the best is *Lonicera heckrottii*, its flowers rose with buff interiors and a slightly glaucous foliage that lasts into December. It is somewhat fragrant at night. But my choice would be the common European honeysuckle, *L. periclymenum* in the form known as "late Dutch." It is vaguely rose-colored, and scented. Tangling with it (planted on the other side of the arch), I would grow the wild American scarlet honeysuckle, *L. sempervirens*, which is scentless.

If I wanted a heavier foliage to make a more monumental entrance, I would choose the wild Japanese clematis, *Clematis maximowicziana*, long known as *C. paniculata*, with white almond-scented stars in great masses at Labor Day, and foliage immune to bugs and blights. To the sides of the arch, forming a screen from the street, I would use a mixture of evergreen and deciduous shrubs. A good fat bush of the English box near the arch would emphasize the entrance, and I might indulge myself here in a variegated yucca and a daslirion from our own Southwest, *D. texanum*, opposite the most dwarf and slowest growing yews, only two or three of them, and perhaps three hollies, *Ilex* "Foster No. 2," and a sweet olive, *Osmanthus* "Gulftide." I would prefer the sweet olive of the Gulf Coast, *O. fragrans*, but it will not grow in Washington.

I might include a large white azalea, the Glenn Dale hybrid, "Treasure," which does not have the fine glossy foliage of the white "Glacier," but which I prefer to other white azaleas.

If there is enough sun, I would include a rose, the old alba variety called "Celeste," which blooms only in May and makes a plant five feet tall and wide. A fine viburnum for the end of the screen is *Viburnum plicatum* "Mariesii" which makes a globe of eight feet, its densely white flowers strung solid along the tabular branches. It is scentless, but is as beautiful as the native dogwood, and blooms four or five days after the dogwoods.

Another viburnum for this screen is the strongly perfumed *V.* × *juddii*, with pink tennis balls of flower that, if the day is soft and mild, can be smelled fifteen feet away. I would also try very hard to find space for a witch hazel, such as the hybrid "Jelena," with orange-bronze flowers beginning in late January and beautiful fall coloring to the leaves. I admit, however, this plant likes to spread out horizontally more than I like. All these shrubs would be planted four or five feet back from the sidewalk, the space being filled in with daffodils and various wild tulips. Along the walk itself, the barrenwort or *Epimedium* makes a flawless and weedproof edging that needs only to be cut to the ground once a year in February. It is dense and polished enough to take the curse off the maturing (that is, dying) leaves of spring bulbs. A plant or two of the Chinese forget-me-not, *Cynoglossum*, which blooms in brilliant gentian blue for six weeks is also useful, as its large leaves come after the early bulbs are through flowering and helps to disguise their undignified ripening.

All these shrubs will require sensible attention as they merge together into a screen. Such an arrangement is no good for the gardener who wants to plant something and then forget it. But such a screen gives an agreeable—I almost said thrilling—variety of greens and textures, with bits of color in late winter and spring and a bit of fragrance as the year goes along.

The walk from sidewalk to house may be concrete, and if so it should be repaved with brick, stone, or slate. It should be six feet wide at least, and edged with barrenworts on one side, to give a neat, cared-for look. On the other side I would use the blue star flower, *Ipheion uniflorum*, sometimes called *Brodiaea* or *Triteleia*. This little South American bulb forms hummocks of narrow, strap-shaped leaves surmounted by dozens of sky-blue stars an inch and a half wide, fragrant, and borne on individual stems. It blooms for three or four weeks starting in mid-March, then dies down for the year.

On both sides of the walk, I would use some fat box bushes, the kind wrongly called "English Box," and an occasional vertical columnar box of the kind wrongly called "American Upright Box." The fat box bushes would be just on one side, only three of them, nothing too studied.

Back of the box, and clearly visible between them, I would carpet the ground with bulbs that bloom early, crocuses (especially the ones bred from *Crocus chrysanthus*) and the very early lavender, flame-centered *C. sieberi*, along with *Chionodoxa sardensis* and *C. gigantea*, *Scilla siberica*, *Endymion hispanicus*, *Scilla tubergeniana*, *Tulipa clusiana*, blue Roman hyacinths and, of course, plenty of snowdrops, the plain *Galanthus nivalis* being best. If I knew where to acquire it, I would also have a patch of *Scilla autumnalis* for September, a modest flower I greatly loved when I once had it from the Rhone Valley. If I decided on a bit of October color, I would choose the blue *Crocus speciosus*.

In this patch of bulbs, which would be left alone after flowering except to keep down the wonderful assortment of chest-high weeds that flourish so well in semi-shaded spots, there is no reason I could not have a few Virginia bluebells *(Mertensia virginica)* and some of the smaller daffodils, but nothing larger than the pale, flared flowers of "Beryl."

Narcissus cyclamineus is perfect, provided I wait a few years for them to seed themselves into colonies. And I would not want to be without at least a couple of patches of trout lilies (*Erythronium* "White Beauty" is as good and as easy as any). All these and even more—surely I would not omit *Fritillaria meleagris*, sometimes called the toad lily, with its checkered nodding bells—can be got into a space less than twenty feet square.

Back of the box on the other side of the walk I would have drifts of the daffodils "February Gold" and "Tete-a-Tete." These bloom usually in mid-March and last a month. Bordering the front garden at the sides, behind these bulbs, I might have *Nandina domestica*, not that nasty little speckled dwarf form which is ugly, but the usual five-foot-high kind with beautiful divided leaves and great panicles of scarlet berries. Not in a row or a hedge, just a good clump of it, along with the glossy evergreen photinia, maybe a few barberries, a fine fat bush of *Euonymus alata* "Compacta" for its dusky but brilliant red fall leaves, *Viburnum wrightii* and *V. setigerum*, which would be happier in full sun but which make do with light woodland conditions, and near the house, the relatively small crab, *Malus sargentii*. If I had more space I would instead plant the tea crab, *Malus hupehensis*. These two are better than other crabs.

The house has a small gabled entrance supported by four posts. In front of them and to the side I would try the common blue hydrangeas that everybody grows. They bloom in June and announce their need for water by drooping leaves. A plant I greatly love is the little bamboo about mid-thigh in height, *Shibataea kumasasa*, which is evergreen but which sometimes browns at the edges in a cold winter. It runs a little, but behaves better than most bamboos. If there were more sun at one end of the little porch I'd plant the somewhat tender Mexican orange, *Choisya ternata*, which is not an orange at all. For the posts, which I would not allow to become completely covered, I would plant the madly vigorous April-blooming pink *Clematis* × *vedrariensis*, leading it horizontally on

catenary garlands or else letting it loose on the porch roof. Another post I would devote to the sumptuous but small-flowered clematis, "Etoile Violette," which will make a ball of flowers two feet wide and three feet high at eye level if given wire support to six feet and no higher. Another post would be devoted to the slightly tender *Smilax smallii* and yet another to the Japanese clematis mentioned earlier. This will make a fine mass of foliage and will stay in bounds if its wire support is seven feet high. Otherwise it will romp on up to twenty or thirty feet, and I want all these vines to decorate and by no means obscure their little columns, an effect ensured by discreet snipping at them off and on through the year.

In the main garden behind the house I would have a brick walk, five feet wide and perfectly straight, with a couple of upright yews, *Taxus* × *media* "Hicksii," on one side. The dark green yews would support the white clematis, "Henryi," and a pink rambler rose, "Mrs. F. W. Flight," which apparently nobody in the world likes except me and the Roseraie de la Haye in Paris. We both think it superb.

The walk would have five arches over it, about fifteen feet apart, covered with roses of the kind hardly anybody grows nowadays. On the first one (with one of the tall yews at one side of the arch) there would be the white rambler, "Seagull," on one side and a bush of the common red rugosa rose, "Hansa," on the other. Growing into the rose and yew and mingling with the rambler rose I would have the small clematis, "Venosa Violacea," which blooms at the same time. The next arch I would devote to "Aglaia," which is yellow, and "Violette." The two do not bloom together, and "Violette" is scentless.

The next arch would be covered by "Blairii No. 2," a rather plain name for an opulent old Bourbon rose decked out in fat, pink, perfumed flowers rimmed in pale blush. It is too big a plant for an arch, but if I want it there, who should complain? Mingling with it is another "Violette" which overlaps in bloom only three days or so. The next arch is more sober, given entirely to the white hybrid musk, "Moonlight," and the last arch is devoted to the single, changeable China rose called "Mutabilis." It is not a climber, but will cover an eight-foot-high arch. It is a trifle tender to cold and should be planted against a wall, where it will easily grow to ten feet or more. If it proves too susceptible to being killed back on the arch, it will remain as a bush on each side and the arch clothed with that best of the larger flowered clematis, "Perle d'Azur."

I see that at this rate every reader will doze off long before we finish the garden. I have said nothing of so many plants that I would not willingly live without, and shall speak of them briefly.

Irises are the most beautiful of all flowers, best grown in solid beds with nothing else. I should want at least one bed of them, in pastels, with only a few deep blues and purples and no reds, bronzes, or blacks, but plenty of straw yellow and other yellows, blues and lavenders, and light raspberry or soft magenta—a color of critical importance in bringing out the full beauty of the yellows and blues.

Poppies and cornflowers, larkspurs and nasturtiums, petunias of a semi-wild type, such as you see along alleys, off-white and off-lavender and smelling sweet at night, are flowers I would have every year.

Other indispensable roses not yet mentioned are the great climber, the pink "Mme. Gregoire Staechelin," and the wild-looking white rambler, "Polyantha Grandiflora," sometimes called *Rosa gentiliana.* The modest-in-height climber, "Blossomtime," with intensely fragrant, pink hybrid-tea-type blooms all summer is one of the few modern roses I would grow. They are all right, but when space is limited I would not find room for them. I would always grow the purple gallica roses, "Cardinal de Richelieu" and "Tuscany," just out of habit, and the small flowered "Blush Noisette" out of passion. I mentioned it once, why not again? The great Noisette climber, "Jaune Desprez," comes close to being my idea of a perfect rose, and I wonder how many gardeners who are fussing about with the newest climbers would prefer this old one, so silky in texture, so supreme in scent, so delicate in its blend of flesh, rose, canary, buff and a touch of orange, if they knew it existed. Then there is "Jacques Cartier," a steady bloomer finely scented, a good healthy bush with quartered flowers of baby pink, and the great white climber, "Mme. Alfred Carriere." These are all roses, from among so many hundred, that I would have in my garden.

I love vines. The only grape, of a dozen or so I have tried, that produces what I consider edible grapes is "Villard Blanc," but any grape at all can be justified for its beautiful foliage. Another climber that is nothing much in flower (though it has blue duck-egg fruits in late summer) but unsurpassed for delicate green foliage is *Akebia quinata*. Sometimes an arch is better served by this Asian vine that has no flowers to speak of than by a vine of flashy flowers that lacks the elegant disease-proof leaves.

I do not want to go through life without *Polygonum aubertii*, with racemes of white, lightly perfumed flowers blooming almost all summer, although I know well how troublesome it is to keep in bounds. Ideally, I would grow it up a dying forest tree and let it reach for the stars.

Yet another beautiful vine I must have is the Carolina jessamine, with wonderfully sweet little yellow trumpets in April. And few vines please me better than trumpet vines, relished by hummingbirds above all others, and of these I would have to have both *Campsis* "Mme. Galen," a larger flowered hybrid of our wayside native trumpet vine, and the yellow trumpet vine, which is very solid yellow—hummingbirds love it, despite the absence of any red.

There must be big agaves (*Agave americana* in its white and yellow variegated forms) in pots or tubs, and a couple of blue Nile lilies (*Agapanthus*) as well. Tuberoses—the "Mexican Single" is the best—are indispensable but a royal nuisance as they are not hardy in Washington over winter, and they are trouble to dig up and plant out every year.

Of annual flowers, few give so much for so little labor as the moon vine or *Ipomoea alba* (syn. *Calonyction*) which romps about for twenty feet or so. I would not willingly live with a chain link fence, but if I had to (say, a gun at my head) I would plant moon vines for summer.

Another plant of great and refined beauty I must have is *Kadsura japonica*, a delicate twiner with leaves smaller than but otherwise rather similar to those of *Magnolia grandiflora*. It has small, white, inconspicuous, magnolia-type flowers and red fruit, but it is for its foliage I would grow it. It deserves a sheltered but very prominent place—not just stuck in somewhere—where it can be seen against mellow old brick or stone or first-rate wrought iron, not that anybody has that any more.

Whatever sacrifice is necessary, there must be a fish pool. Common red goldfish are quite beautiful enough, and it should be as large as possible so I will not go mad trying to choose among the endless beautiful water lilies. Among tropicals, I would have *Nymphaea gigantea*, and the hybrids "Blue Beauty," "August Koch," and "Daubeniana"—all of them blue. The white "Juno" is the best of night bloomers. Among hardy water lilies the yellow "Chromatella" and the pygmy "Helvola" are the best yellows, though I remember how I once saved my money to buy "Sunrise" when it was new and supposedly so much finer. Of pink, hardy kinds the best to my mind is *N.* × *laydeckeri* "Rosea," which is never more than four inches across its lovely flowers, but there are many of them. All the others I can take or leave alone; there is no such thing as an ugly kind. Of lotus, the best one is the common Asian *Nelumbo nucifera* and I would surely have it.

Of perennials, there are so many it is hard to choose. Certainly the Russian sage, *Perovskia*, and certainly daylilies, including the wild *Hemerocallis citrina* which is fragrant, with long narrow trumpets blooming only at night. Lady's mantle and catmint are in the forefront of easy, useful perennials for placing near a walk.

Peonies (including tree peonies and the gorgeous very early, hybrid red peony, "Red Charm") I would have. Among the main-season peonies, I would never neglect the silver-pink "Mons. Jules Elie" or the crimson-flecked white "Festiva Maxima." The Japanese single peonies are among the best, in such varieties as the soft pink "Westerner" and the deep rose "Largo."

Lilies are the glory of late June. The white "Black Dragon" offers tremendous fragrant trumpets on stems six or seven feet high, and the "Golden Clarion" strain is almost as impressive in rich yellow. I would not have the Asiatic hybrids, but the pink speciosum types would be represented by a large clump, and where I had almost full shade but strong light I would plant the big, gold-striped auratums, especially "Silver Imperial." These grow readily from seed, I have noticed.

I would learn to live without magnolias in a small garden, probably, except maybe *Magnolia stellata* "Rubra," if I could find it again—a rich rose color, not red. But I would have to have a pink locust, maybe the wild American *Robinia kelseyi* or the cultivated variety, "Monument." And a fig, "Brown Turkey," since the little "Celeste" seems not to grow well in Washington.

There is a feeling, I notice, that respectable people do not grow bananas. I have grown several kinds, all marvelous (I speak of the beauty of the plants and do not count on fruit), and would certainly have at least three or four kinds. Another passion is crinums, and at the very least I would insist on the beautiful pink "Cecil Houdyshel."

In fall nothing is more beautiful than the Japanese anemone. The plain single white one is the best. A neglected (but not by me) perennial is the Italian arum, which emerges with calla-like leaves in October. It is blotched with gray-white and is a beautiful surprise all winter, then dies down in June. It is a plant I would want every gardener to enjoy.

What can be said of daffodils, except I would like a great many. The greatest daffodil I have known is "Ceylon," yellow with red cup, but the ones that seize my heart are the late whites with small cups. And surely there would be space for a row of the little perfumed jonquils, such as every southern gardener has, just for cutting. I would not be without "Dawn" and a couple of the old tazetta kinds, which are so happy in sun-baked spots (often found near the garage) interplanted with rain lilies (*Habranthus tubispathus*) and winter-blooming Algerian irises (*Iris unguicularis*).

When I think of so many other wonderful plants I have loved and of all the ones I don't know at all—not yet—I do not see how any garden except the great garden we call the Earth can hold them all, but the few I have mentioned are among those I would bestir myself to plant before the furniture had been unloaded at a new place. And needless to say if I should fetch up in some dwelling without any garden at all, it would not bother me much. I began gardening with nasturtiums in my mother's discarded cold cream jars, and with sweet potatoes in a jar of water. And very satisfactory they were too. And are.

If I Were To Make a Garden

Ernest H. Wilson

 F I WERE to make a garden, another garden, a new garden, I should probably make mistakes as I have done in the past, mistakes like every reader of this has made and will make. There is no royal road or clean-cut path to the making of a garden. It depends so much on circumstances, on area, on climate, on the topography of the site and on the soil. One should, of course, have ideals, but one must always realize that they are ideals and that practice can only approximate to them. I live in New England, where the country is broken and rocky and where conditions for making gardens are very favorable, so it is perhaps best for the purpose that our garden be made there.

Let us assume I have the privilege of selecting the site. In which case, I should want my house, other things being equal, situated on the highest point. Nearby I would have woodland and water—river or lake. Area would be of less importance than situation. The garden should be large, the house small, of cottage type built of old brick. My garden should be about the house, flanking the lawn, and vistas should open through the woodland, and lead down to the water. Having secured the site, I would engage an engineer and the best naturalistic landscape gardener that I could find. Between them they would provide me with a topographical map and a general plan of the whole area. Armed with these I would consider the task myself, for a garden is a personal thing and one's own taste should prevail.

My ambition would be to humor nature and invoke the grace of congruity. Unity without uniformity should be the keynote and the design so wrought that the garden should blend into the landscape around. In other words, I would have a natural garden, not an exotic garden. And what do I mean by this? I mean briefly that I would have a collection of the most beautiful hardy trees, shrubs, vines and flowers that I could procure for the space at my disposal. I would have these so planted and tended that they would seem indigenous in their homes. I would have them so arranged that each could be admired for its individual merits and, not only so, but mutually enhance the charms of its neighbors by contrast or by combination. The transition from the lawn and garden to the woodland and to the landscape beyond should be gradual.

There must, of course, be variety and this should be of the best quality. About the house no foundation-planting of sombre Spruce or Pine, Fir or Hemlock, Arborvitae or Retinospora should obtain. On the east, south and southwest aspects, so far as circumstances permitted, a wide border, irregular in outline, filled with all that is best among herbaceous perennials should range from the windows toward the lawn: stately Hollyhock and Foxglove, Delphinium and Madonna Lily, Shirley and Oriental Poppies, Monkshood and Phlox, Peonies and Iris, Aster and Chrysanthemum in variety, Polyanthus and other Primroses steeped in Forget-me-nots, tender Heliotrope and Jasmine Tobacco. These with any and every other blossom of good color should grow cheek by jowl in my flower border. Thickly they should stand so that as the blossoms faded others would immediately take their place. On one corner of the house Wistaria should climb, and here a Rose and there a climbing Honeysuckle peep in at the window. A garden of sweet odors should live beneath my windows. And somewhere in this border in a sheltered nook a clump of Christmas Rose and Bloodroot should find a home. The tenants of this border should be so selected that from the blush of spring, when Winter Aconite, Snowdrop, Grape-Hyacinth, Squill and Crocus should cheer me, until the frosts turned brown late Asters and Chrysanthemums, my border would be a riot of color. In late November I would put it to bed snugly beneath a covering of leafmold and stable-dung, happy in the knowledge that in the following spring would recommence the wealth of blossom.

Did climate permit, a couple of billowy Boxwood or dwarf Japanese Yew should guard the front-door portals. On the west and north lowgrowing shrubs, both deciduous and evergreen, should have their place. Pink-blossomed *Rhododendron carolinianum* and Azaleas should be grouped with bright-stemmed Dogwood *(Cornus stolonifera)*, Andromeda *(Pieris floribunda)*, and Inkberry *(Ilex glabra)*; *Viburnum Carlesii* should also have a place nearby. By planting the evergreens on the shady side of the house I would guard against the damaging effects of King Sol's strong rays in February and early March and I would enjoy color in season and restful green throughout the year. Beneath this planting there would be bulbs in variety. Color in spring, color in summer, color in autumn and color in winter should be my ambition.

A broad lawn leading toward the woodland should be deluged on its outskirts with Narcissus of every form, and nearer the house Crocus and Squills should be allowed to dot the skirts of the lawn. I hold with that greatest of living gardeners, William Robinson, that the lawn is the heart of the garden and the happiest thing there is in it and I believe that there should be in front of every home a piece of green grass, as spacious as means permit, well-mowed, well-rolled and kept free from worm and weed. Flowers may come and leaves may go but a well-kept lawn goes on forever. It refreshes the spirit through the eye, which never tires. It is most to be admired when it imperceptibly fades into the beyond where ancient trees, Oak, Elm, Hickory, Beech, Maple, White Pine and Hemlock spread themselves.

Flanking the lawn and swinging in a semi-circle about the house, shrubs should be planted, not mixed together as an impenetrable screen, but individually, so that each could show its charms to best advantage. Here should grow bright Goldenbell, fragrant Mock-orange, floriferous Spiraea, Pearl Bush, berried Barberry, Cotoneaster and bush Honeysuckles. Gray-leaved, pink-blossomed, *Lonicera Korolkowii*, and that most delightful of shrubs, the Beautybush *(Kolkwitzia amabilis)*, should occupy central portions. Also prominent should be those fountains of yellow and white Roses—Father Hugh's—and its white counterpart, *Rosa spinosissima altaica*. Lilacs I would have in clumps, but not the modern French hybrids. My fancy runs to the fragrant, old-fashioned white and colored forms, and as isolated bushes there should be Persian and Rouen Lilacs. Somewhere near the house, for its fragrance, should be grown that charming Lilac, *Syringa pubescens*, and the old Syringa *philadelphus coronarius*.

The guiding spirit in selecting my shrubs should be not merely blossom in due season but berries of bright colors in the autumn. For this reason bush Honeysuckles, Barberries and Cotoneasters should play a prominent part. On fence, trellis and pillar, Clematis of varied colors and Roses in pink and white and red should ramble, and I would have as many as space allowed. The modern Hybrid Tea and the Hybrid Perpetual demand too much to find a place, a prominent place, in the garden I would build. Old-fashioned Scotch Roses there should be and fragrant Sweet Briar, nor should certain simple Roses of the countryside be omitted. The seashore Rose *(Rosa virginiana)* and that of the prairie *(R. setigera)* should have prominence. Some of the bolder upthrust rocks should remain unclad since they embolden the landscape. On others, evergreens, *Evonymus radicans*, should cling, and over others *R. Wichuraiana* and its descendants and Bittersweet *(Celastrus articulatus)* should sprawl; elsewhere *Cotoneaster horizontalis* should be allowed to spread its flattened, sail-like branches decked with scarlet in the autumn and early winter. In full sun beyond the lawn, Heather in white and purple should be planted and encouraged to form pure swards. In shady nooks, Ferns in variety and Lily-of-the-Valley should find a home.

Trees do not make a garden but a garden without trees scarcely deserves its name. Depending on the area available I would plant somewhere in view of the house a Yew tree, a Ginkgo, the fountain-like Linden *(Tilia petiolaris)*, a Tulip tree for its noble, handsome foliage and unique flower and the Yulan Magnolias in white and pink. Crabapples would be essential, both for their beauty of blossoms and fruit and as food for the birds in winter. Somewhere near the house I would have the Rosebud Cherry, its weeping branches strung with pink, and its round-topped relative, *Prunus subhirtella*, of which no tree in spring is more delightful. Beyond a Sargent Cherry should rear its beauty. Were a hedge necessary in the scheme of things it should be, if near the house, of Japanese Yew. If well beyond, to shut out buildings, of Canadian Hemlock.

As I have said before, the margin of my lawn should be drenched with bulbs, the Poet's Narcissus, trumpet-flowered Jonquils, and common Daffydowndillies. Could it be arranged, a wall of stone or old brick with a dry ditch beneath should separate lawn from meadow and woodland, and in this wall Aubrietia, prostrate Phlox, Wallflowers, Sun Roses, Sandworts, Sedums and indeed, anything and everything that could be encouraged to grow should find a home. Flowers! flowers! should be the cry and wherever it is possible for them to flourish they should have their chance.

Ask a small boy what he thinks a garden is for and his answer will probably be, "Strawberries." And no one will deny but that Strawberries are a very delightful product of the garden and what vegetables are so fresh, so sweet and so delicious as those culled from one's own patch. And, so, my garden should have its vegetable patch and this should be as large as circumstances permitted. It should be open and unencumbered by trees of any sort. If practical, a wall should surround it and on this wall would grow trained trees of Apple, Pear, Peach and other stone fruits. A Strawberry bed should have its proper place and so should every vegetable which the skill of the gardener has made available. But somewhere in this garden there should be a good space set aside where flowers for cutting would be planted in abundance. Here annuals of all sorts should have their place, with Gladiolus, Gypsophylla, Cosmos and Sweet Peas. In planting this area for cutting, the effort would be to supply the house with all its needs from early summer until late fall. This walled garden should be hidden from the house by conifers and approached by a curving path. I dislike gravel to walk upon and wherever possible none but grass paths should prevail.

My woods should be so thinned that trunk of Birch and Pine, Hickory and Maple could be seen to best advantage, and in this wood Flowering Dogwood, with Mountain Laurel *(Kalmia latifolia)* and *Rhododendron maximum* should be grouped in bold clumps. A moist place should accommodate the fragrant *Magnolia glauca* and wild flowers and ferns should have full freedom.

In some corner of my garden I should want seclusion, some quiet retreat where I could retire and rest apart from the world and beyond the reach of every visitor, a sort of *sanctum sanctorum* where only family and self had free access. A garden can be anything we like to make it and I would strive to have it filled with all that is best in herb and vine, shrub and tree. Ah! me, what fun there is in planning a garden.

A NOTE ABOUT

All of the illustrations in the book are adapted from the covers of garden books published in the United States and England between 1894 and 1930. Except for the colors, with which I have taken many liberties, the designs have not been altered significantly except to accommodate the size of the page. I hope my artwork pays adequate tribute to the beauty of the originals.

I can identify only two of the many artists who created covers. Margaret Armstrong was one of the best-known and most prolific designers in the field, flourishing between 1891–

TITLE PAGE:

THE PRUNING MANUAL by Liberty Hyde Bailey
The Macmillan Company, 1921
Cover artist: W

COPYRIGHT PAGE:

GARDENING FOR LITTLE GIRLS
by Olive Hyde Foster
Duffield & Company, 1917

ACKNOWLEDGMENTS, CONTENTS, FOREWORD:

COLOUR IN MY GARDEN by Louise Beebe Wilder
Doubleday, Doran & Company, Inc., 1930

DEDICATION:

WILD FLOWERS AND STATE FLOWERS OF NORTH AMERICA by Lydia Northrop Gilbert
George Sully & Company, Inc., 1930

ENDPAPERS:

GARDEN PORTRAITS by Amelia Leavitt Hill
Robert M. McBride & Company, 1923

THE ILLUSTRATIONS

1913. She created over three hundred book covers of exceptional beauty. When her covers are identified, it is by the initials MA. Amy Richards, active between 1896–1918, likewise contracted her initials into a stylized AR. While the others remain anonymous, some left behind an initial or monogram, which is not always legible in a well-worn book. But research has begun, and perhaps more of these unsung artists will be recognized in the future.

Following is a list of the editions I consulted.

CHAPTER OPENERS AND ADDITIONAL ILLUSTRATIONS:

Page 11
THE GARDEN OF A COMMUTER'S WIFE
by Mabel Osgood Wright
The Macmillan Company, 1904

Page 15
GARDENS OF THE GREAT MUGHALS
by Constance Mary Villiers-Stuart
Adam & Charles Black, 1913

Page 21
A FEW FAMILIAR FLOWERS by Margaret Warner Morley
Ginn and Company, Publishers, 1903

Page 29
GARDENING FOR BEGINNERS by Ernest Thomas Cook
Charles Scribner's Sons, 1901

Page 32
WESTERN WILD FLOWERS by Margaret Armstrong
G.P. Putnam's Sons, 1915
Cover Artist: presumably Margaret Armstrong

A Note about the Illustrations

Page 35
THE GARDEN, YOU AND I by Mabel Osgood Wright
The Macmillan Company, 1906

Page 37
THE WELL-CONSIDERED GARDEN by Mrs. Francis King
Charles Scribner's Sons, 1915

Page 39
OLD TIME GARDENS by Alice Morse Earle
The Macmillan Company, 1901

Page 42
GARDENS OF ENGLAND by Ernest Thomas Cook
A. & C. Black Ltd., 1923
Cover artist: Ⓣ

Page 49
HOW TO KNOW THE WILD FLOWERS
by Mrs. William Starr Dana
Charles Scribner's Sons, 1894

Page 57
NATURE'S GARDEN by Neltje Blanchan
Doubleday, Page & Co., 1900
(also used for the cover)

Page 61
A GUIDE TO THE WILD FLOWERS by Alice Lounsberry
Frederick A. Stokes Company, 1899
Cover Artist: Amy Richards

Page 64
ACCORDING TO SEASON by Frances Theodora Parsons
Charles Scribner's Sons, 1902
Cover Artist: Margaret Armstrong

A Note about the Illustrations

Page 71

DAFFODILS, NARCISSUS AND HOW TO GROW THEM
by A.M. Kirby
Doubleday, Page & Co., 1907

Page 74

EVERY WOMAN'S FLOWER GARDEN by Mary Hampden
Duffield & Company, 1915

Page 79

A WOMAN'S HARDY GARDEN by Helena Rutherfurd Ely
The Macmillan Company, 1913
Cover artist: identified by illegible monogram
(also used for folio decorations)

Page 85

BEAUTIFUL FLOWERS AND HOW TO GROW THEM
by Horace J. Wright and Walter P. Wright
T.C. & E.C. Jack Ltd., 1930

Page 88

TAMING THE WILDINGS by Herbert Durand
G.P. Putnam's Sons, 1923

Page 93

THE GARDEN MAGAZINE (Bound volumes)
Doubleday, Page & Co., 1900

A NOTE ABOUT THE ILLUSTRATIONS:
SCOTTISH GARDENS by Sir Herbert Maxwell
Edward Arnold, 1911

COLOPHON:
CONTINUOUS BLOOM IN AMERICA by Louise Shelton
Charles Scribner's Sons, 1928
Cover artist: GE

Designed by Diana M. Jones
Composed in Cloister Old Style
by Trufont Typographers, Inc.,
Hicksville, New York
Printed and bound by
Arnoldo Mondadori Editore S.p.A.,
Verona, Italy